REPORT OF THE RIVER MASTER OF THE DELAWARE RIVER

FOR THE PERIOD
DECEMBER 1, 2005–NOVEMBER 30, 2006

Open-File Report 2011–1177

U.S. Department of the Interior
U.S. Geological Survey

CALENDAR FOR REPORT YEAR 2006

DECEMBER 2005

S	M	T	W	T	F	S
				1	2	3
4	5	6	7	8	9	10
11	12	13	14	15	16	17
18	19	20	21	22	23	24
25	26	27	28	29	30	31

JANUARY 2006

S	M	T	W	T	F	S
1	2	3	4	5	6	7
8	9	10	11	12	13	14
15	16	17	18	19	20	21
22	23	24	25	26	27	28
29	30	31				

FEBRUARY

S	M	T	W	T	F	S
			1	2	3	4
5	6	7	8	9	10	11
12	13	14	15	16	17	18
19	20	21	22	23	24	25
26	27	28				

MARCH

S	M	T	W	T	F	S
			1	2	3	4
5	6	7	8	9	10	11
12	13	14	15	16	17	18
19	20	21	22	23	24	25
26	27	28	29	30	31	

APRIL

S	M	T	W	T	F	S
						1
2	3	4	5	6	7	8
9	10	11	12	13	14	15
16	17	18	19	20	21	22
23	24	25	26	27	28	29
30						

MAY

S	M	T	W	T	F	S
	1	2	3	4	5	6
7	8	9	10	11	12	13
14	15	16	17	18	19	20
21	22	23	24	25	26	27
28	29	30	31			

JUNE 2006

S	M	T	W	T	F	S
				1	2	3
4	5	6	7	8	9	10
11	12	13	14	15	16	17
18	19	20	21	22	23	24
25	26	27	28	29	30	

JULY

S	M	T	W	T	F	S
						1
2	3	4	5	6	7	8
9	10	11	12	13	14	15
16	17	18	19	20	21	22
23	24	25	26	27	28	29
30	31					

AUGUST

S	M	T	W	T	F	S
		1	2	3	4	5
6	7	8	9	10	11	12
13	14	15	16	17	18	19
20	21	22	23	24	25	26
27	28	29	30	31		

SEPTEMBER

S	M	T	W	T	F	S
					1	2
3	4	5	6	7	8	9
10	11	12	13	14	15	16
17	18	19	20	21	22	23
24	25	26	27	28	29	30

OCTOBER

S	M	T	W	T	F	S
1	2	3	4	5	6	7
8	9	10	11	12	13	14
15	16	17	18	19	20	21
22	23	24	25	26	27	28
29	30	31				

NOVEMBER

S	M	T	W	T	F	S
			1	2	3	4
5	6	7	8	9	10	11
12	13	14	15	16	17	18
19	20	21	22	23	24	25
26	27	28	29	30		

Report of the River Master of the Delaware River for the period December 1, 2005–November 30, 2006

By Bruce E. Krejmas, Gary N. Paulachok, and Stephen F. Blanchard

Open-File Report 2011–1177

U.S. Department of the Interior
U.S. Geological Survey

U.S. Department of the Interior
KEN SALAZAR, Secretary

U.S. Geological Survey
Marcia K. McNutt, Director

U.S. Geological Survey, Reston, Virginia: 2011

For more information about the USGS and its products:
Telephone: 1–888–ASK–USGS
World Wide Web: http://www.usgs.gov/

Suggested citation:
Krejmas, B.E., Paulachok, G.N., and Blanchard, S.F., 2010, Report of the River Master of the Delaware River for the period December 1, 2005–November 30, 2006: U.S. Geological Survey Open-File Report 2011–1177, 79 p.

Contents

Figures

Tables

Conversion Factors and Vertical Datum

Multiply	By	To obtain
Length		
inch (in.)	25.4	millimeter (mm)
foot (ft)	0.3048	meter (m)
mile (mi)	1.609	kilometer (km)
Area		
square mile (mi^2)	2.590	square kilometer (km^2)
Volume		
million gallons (Mgal)	3,785	cubic meter (m^3)
million gallons (Mgal)	1.547	cubic foot per second day (ft^3/s)-d
billion gallons (Bgal)	3.785	cubic hectometer (hm^3)
cubic foot per second day (ft^3/s)-d	0.002447	cubic hectometer (hm^3)
Flow rate		
million gallons per day (Mgal/d)	1.547	cubic foot per second (ft^3/s)
million gallons per day (Mgal/d)	0.04381	cubic meter per second (m^3/s)
billion gallons per day (Bgal/d)	43.81	cubic meter per second (m^3/s)
cubic foot per second (ft^3/s)	0.02832	cubic meter per second (m^3/s)

Datum: Vertical coordinate information is referenced to the North American Vertical Datum of 1988. Horizontal coordinate information is referenced to the North American Datum of 1983.

Elevation, as used in this report, refers to the distance above a vertical datum.

Temperature in degrees Celsius (°C) may be converted to degrees Fahrenheit (°F) as follows: °F=(1.8x°C)+32

CHEMICAL CONCENTRATIONS

In this report, concentrations of chloride and dissolved oxygen are given in milligrams per liter (mg/L). Milligrams per liter represents the mass of solute (milligrams) per unit volume (liter) of water.

RIVER MASTER LETTER OF TRANSMITTAL AND SPECIAL REPORT

OFFICE OF THE DELAWARE RIVER MASTER
United States Geological Survey
415 National Center
Reston, Virginia 20192

October 12, 2011

The Honorable
John G. Roberts, Jr.
Chief Justice of the United States

The Honorable
Jack A. Markell
Governor of Delaware

The Honorable
Christopher J. Christie
Governor of New Jersey

The Honorable
Andrew M. Cuomo
Governor of New York

The Honorable
Tom Corbett
Governor of Pennsylvania

The Honorable
Michael R. Bloomberg
Mayor of the City of New York

No. 5, Original.—October Term, 1950
State of New Jersey, Complainant,
v.
State of New York and City of New York, Defendants,
Commonwealth of Pennsylvania and State of Delaware, Intervenors.

Dear Sirs:

For the record, and in compliance with the provisions of the Amended Decree of the Supreme Court of the United States entered June 7, 1954, I am hereby transmitting the 53rd Annual Report of the River Master of the Delaware River for the 12-month period from December 1, 2005, to November 30, 2006. In this report, this period is referred to as the River Master report year or the report year.

During the 2006 River Master report year, monthly precipitation in the upper Delaware River Basin ranged from 39 percent of the long-term average in March 2006 to 290 percent of the long-term average in June 2006. Total precipitation during the report year was 11.36 inches (in.) more than the long-term average. Precipitation during the December to May period, when reservoirs typically refill, was 1.08 in.

less than the 65-year average. Precipitation during the report year was below normal in December, February, March, July, and August, and above normal in the other seven months.

On December 1, 2005, when the report year began, combined storage in the New York City reservoirs in the upper Delaware River Basin was 213.173 billion gallons (Bgal) or 78.7 percent of combined storage capacity. Median combined storage on December 1, computed on the basis of 38 years of record, is 177.307 Bgal. In early February, the Decree Parties established temporary spill reduction programs for Pepacton and Neversink Reservoirs. Storage remained above median levels throughout the year. During the report year, operations in the basin were conducted as stipulated by the Decree.

On April 27, 2006, the Delaware River Master Advisory Committee met at the U.S. Geological Survey's (USGS) New Jersey Water Science Center in West Trenton, New Jersey, to discuss hydrologic conditions in the basin and operational procedures for the 2006 reservoir-release season. During the report year, the following individuals served as members of the Advisory Committee:

Delaware	John H. Talley
New Jersey	Samuel A. Wolfe
New York	Sandra Allen
New York City	Michael A. Principe
Pennsylvania	Cathleen Curran Myers

The River Master informed the Advisory Committee that, on the basis of information provided by New York City, the excess-release quantity beginning June 15, 2006, was 8.763 Bgal. Based on reservoir release programs in Delaware River Basin Commission (DRBC) Docket No. D-77-20 CP (Revisions Nos. 7 and 8), the excess-release quantity was to be used for various purposes. In late September, the Decree Parties established a temporary spill reduction program described in DRBC Docket No. D-77-20-CP (Revision 9) for Pepacton, Cannonsville, and Neversink Reservoirs.

During the report year, the River Master and staff participated in a number of water-supply related meetings of the DRBC. The Deputy Delaware River Master met periodically with representatives of the Decree Parties as a member of the Decree Parties Work Group and DRBC's Regulated Flow Advisory Committee. Issues of particular interest to the River Master involved management of reservoir releases and regulated streamflow in the upper Delaware River Basin.

The USGS continued operation of its field office of the Delaware River Master at Milford, Pennsylvania. Gary N. Paulachok, Deputy Delaware River Master, continued in charge of the office, assisted by Bruce E. Krejmas, Hydrologist.

During the year, the River Master's office continued the weekly distribution of a summary hydrologic report. These reports contain provisional data on precipitation in the upper Delaware River Basin, releases and spills from New York City reservoirs to the Delaware River, diversions to the New York City water-supply system, reservoir contents, daily segregation of flow of the Delaware River at the USGS Montague, New Jersey gaging station, and diversions by New Jersey. The reports were distributed to members of the Delaware River Master Advisory Committee and to other parties interested in Delaware River operations. A monthly summary of hydrologic conditions also was provided to Advisory Committee members. The weekly and monthly hydrologic reports were posted on the River Master's Web site.

The first section of this report documents Delaware River operations during the report year. During the year, the City of New York diverted 138.091 Bgal from the Delaware River Basin and released 135.791 Bgal from Pepacton, Cannonsville, and Neversink Reservoirs to the Delaware River. The River Master directed releases from these reservoirs to the Delaware River that totaled 14.248 Bgal.

The second section of this report describes water quality at various monitor sites on the Delaware Estuary. It includes basic data on chemical properties and physical characteristics of the water, and presents summary statistics on the data.

Throughout the year, diversions to New York City's water supply and releases designed to maintain the flow of the Delaware River at Montague were made as directed by the River Master. Diversions by New York City from its reservoirs in the Delaware River Basin did not exceed the limit stipulated by the Decree. Diversions by New Jersey also were within stipulated limits.

The River Master and staff are grateful for the continued cooperation and support of the Decree Parties. Also, the contributions of the PPL Corporation and Mirant Corporation in informing the River Master of plans for power generation and furnishing data on reservoir releases are greatly appreciated.

Sincerely yours,

/Signed/

Stephen F. Blanchard
Delaware River Master

3

DELAWARE RIVER OPERATIONS

Abstract

A Decree of the Supreme Court of the United States, entered June 7, 1954, established the position of Delaware River Master within the U.S. Geological Survey (USGS). In addition, the Decree authorizes diversions of water from the Delaware River Basin and requires compensating releases from certain reservoirs, owned by New York City, to be made under the supervision and direction of the River Master. The Decree stipulates that the River Master will furnish reports to the Court, not less frequently than annually. This report is the 53rd Annual Report of the River Master of the Delaware River. It covers the 2006 River Master report year—the period from December 1, 2005, to November 30, 2006.

During the report year, precipitation in the upper Delaware River Basin was 55.03 inches (in.) or 126 percent of the long-term average. Combined storage in Pepacton, Cannonsville, and Neversink Reservoirs was above the long-term median level on December 1, 2005. Reservoir storage remained above long-term median levels throughout the report year. Delaware River operations during the year were conducted as stipulated by the Decree.

Diversions from the Delaware River Basin by New York City and New Jersey were in full compliance with the Decree. Reservoir releases were made as directed by the River Master at rates designed to meet the flow objective for the Delaware River at Montague, New Jersey, on 27 days during the report year. Releases were made at conservation rates—or rates designed to relieve thermal stress and protect the fishery and aquatic habitat in the tailwaters of the reservoirs—on all other days.

During the report year, New York City and New Jersey complied fully with the terms of the Decree, and directives and requests of the River Master.

As part of a long-term program, the quality of water in the Delaware Estuary between Trenton, New Jersey, and Reedy Island Jetty, Delaware, was monitored at various locations. Data on water temperature, specific conductance, dissolved oxygen, and pH were collected continuously by electronic instruments at four sites. In addition, selected water-quality data were collected at 19 sites on a twice-monthly basis and at 3 sites on a monthly basis.

Introduction

An Amended Decree of the Supreme Court of the United States, entered June 7, 1954, authorized diversions of water from the Delaware River Basin and provided for releases of water from three New York City reservoirs—Pepacton, Cannonsville, and Neversink—to the upper Delaware River. The Decree stipulates that these diversions and releases are to be made under the supervision and direction of the Delaware River Master. The Decree also stipulates that reports on Delaware River operations be made to the Court not less frequently than annually. This report documents operations from December 1, 2005, to November 30, 2006, or the 2006 River Master report year. The report also presents information on the quality of water in the Delaware Estuary during the report year.

Some hydrologic data presented in this report are records of streamflow and water quality for USGS data-collection stations. These records were collected, computed, and furnished by the offices of the

4

USGS at Troy, New York; Exton and New Cumberland, Pennsylvania; and West Trenton, New Jersey, in cooperation with the States of New York and New Jersey, the Commonwealth of Pennsylvania, and the City of New York. The locations of major streams and reservoirs, and selected streamflow-gaging stations in the Delaware River Basin are shown in figure 1.

Acknowledgments

The River Master's daily operation records were prepared from hydrologic data collected chiefly on a day-to-day basis. Data for these records were collected and computed by the Office of the Delaware River Master or were furnished by the following agencies and utilities: Data for Pepacton, Cannonsville, and Neversink Reservoirs by the New York City Department of Environmental Protection, Bureau of Water Supply; for Lake Wallenpaupack by the PPL Corporation; and for Rio Reservoir by Mirant Corporation. Precipitation data and quantitative precipitation forecasts were provided by the National Weather Service (NWS) office in Binghamton, New York.

Definition of Terms and Procedures

The following definitions apply to various terms and procedures used in the operations documented in this report. A table for converting inch-pound units to the International System of Units (SI) is given on page vi.

- **Balancing Adjustment.**—An operating procedure used by the River Master to correct for inaccuracies inherent in the design of releases from New York City reservoirs to meet the Montague flow objective. The balancing adjustment is computed as 10 percent of the difference between the cumulative adjusted directed release and the cumulative directed release required for exact forecasting. The balancing adjustment is applied to the following day's release design. The maximum daily balancing adjustment is intentionally limited to preclude unacceptably large variations in the adjusted flow objective.

- **Capacity.**—Total usable volume in a reservoir between the point of maximum depletion and the elevation of the lowest crest of the spillway.

- **Conservation releases.**—Controlled releases from Pepacton, Cannonsville, and Neversink Reservoirs designed to maintain specified minimum flows in stream channels (tailwaters) below the reservoirs. The conservation rates shown in table 2[1] are defined as follows:

  - **Normal.**—Conservation releases when New York City combined reservoir storage is in the normal operations zone.

  - **Watch.**—Conservation releases when New York City combined reservoir storage is in the drought watch operations zone.

  - **Warning.**—Conservation releases when New York City combined reservoir storage is in the drought warning operations zone.

  - **Drought.**—Conservation releases when New York City combined reservoir storage is in the drought operations zone.

  The combined storage zones for New York City Delaware Basin reservoirs are shown in figure 2.

---

[1]All numbered tables in the section "Delaware River Operations" are grouped at the end of this section, beginning on page 23.

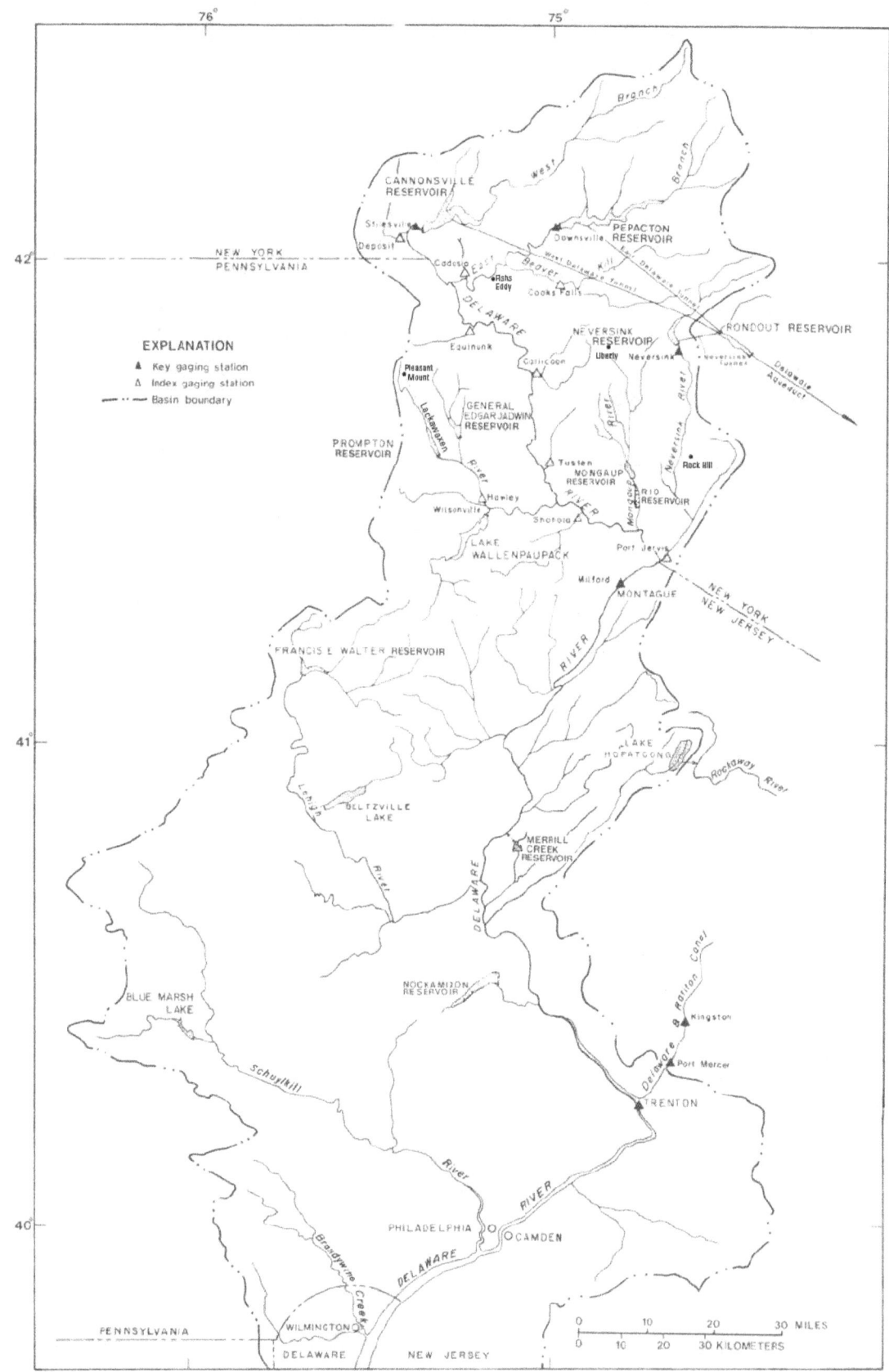

Figure 1. Delaware River Basin above Wilmington, Delaware.

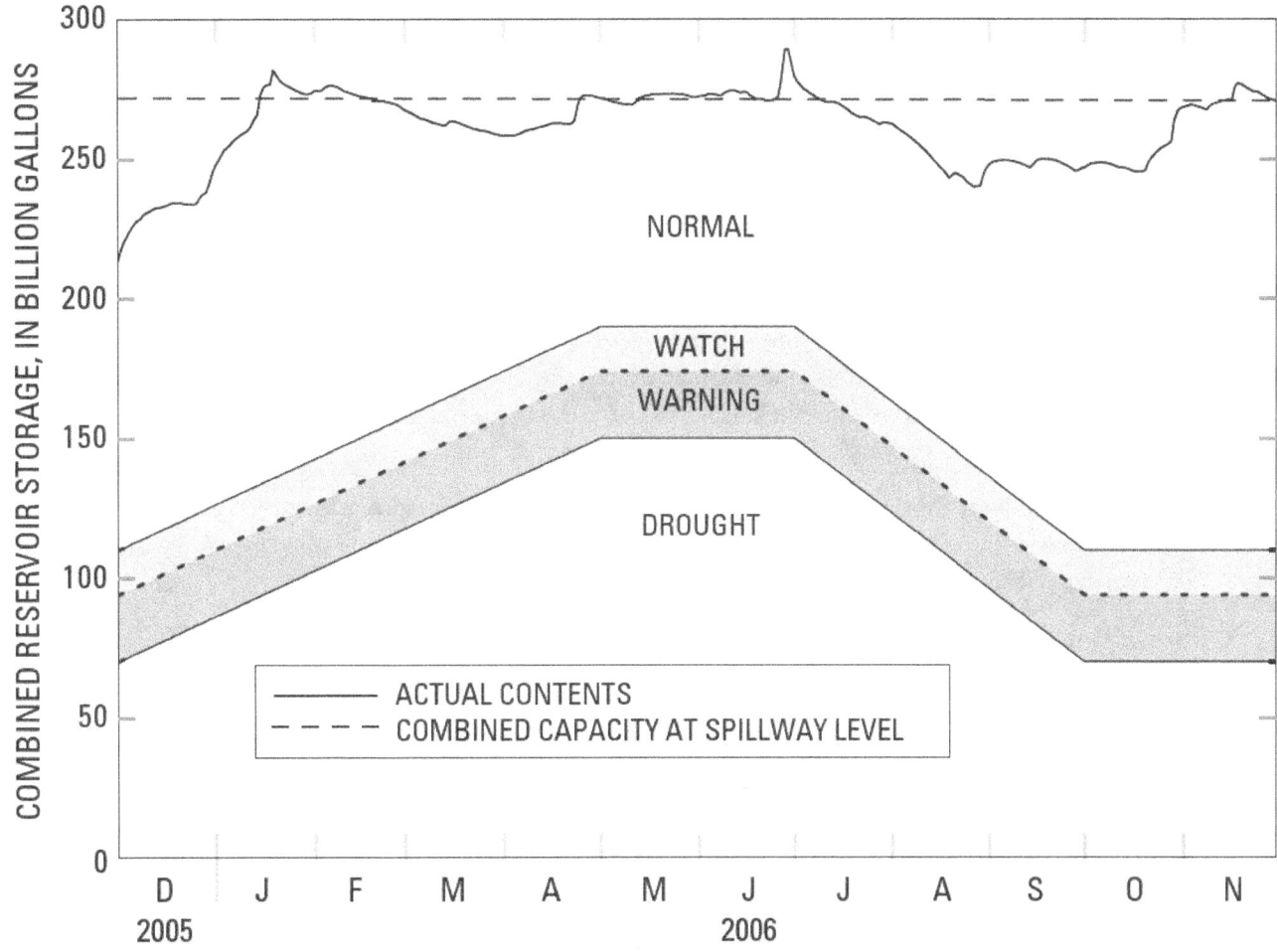

Figure 2. Operation curves and actual contents for New York City reservoirs in the Delaware River Basin, December 1, 2005, to November 30, 2006.

- **Daily excess-release credits**.—Daily credits and deficits during the seasonal release period (June 15 to the following March 15) are computed as the arithmetic difference between the daily mean discharge of the Delaware River at Montague, New Jersey, and 1,750 cubic feet per second (ft³/s). The daily credit cannot exceed the 24-hour period releases from Pepacton, Cannonsville, and Neversink Reservoirs routed to Montague and made in accordance with direction, except as follows: during the seasonal period, credits also are applied for part or all of other releases from these reservoirs that contribute to the daily mean discharge at Montague between 1,750 ft³/s and the applicable excess-release rate.

- **Directed releases**.—Controlled releases from New York City reservoirs in the upper Delaware River Basin, designed by the Delaware River Master to meet the Montague flow objective.

- **Diversions**.—The out-of-basin transfer of water by New York City from Pepacton, Cannonsville, and Neversink Reservoirs in the upper Delaware River Basin through the East Delaware, West Delaware, and Neversink Tunnels, respectively, to the City's water-supply system. Also, the out-of-basin transfer of water by New Jersey from the Delaware River through the Delaware and Raritan Canal.

- **Excess quantity**.—As defined by the Decree, the excess quantity of water is equal to 83 percent of the amount by which the estimated consumption in New York City during the year is less than the City's estimate of continuous safe yield [1,665 million gallons per day (Mgal/d) stipulated by

7

the 1954 Decree] from all its sources of supply obtainable without pumping, except that the excess quantity shall not exceed 70 Bgal. Each year, the seasonal period for release of the excess quantity begins on June 15. The flow objective for the period becomes effective at Montague on that date and remains in effect until the following March 15, or until the cumulative total of excess-release credits equals the applicable excess quantity, whichever occurs first.

- **Index gaging stations.**—Particular sites on tributaries of the upper Delaware River where systematic observations of gage height and discharge are made. These stations are used mainly during the directed-release season to estimate inflows of surface water to the upper Delaware River.

- **Key gaging stations.**—Particular sites on the East Branch Delaware River, West Branch Delaware River, Neversink River, Delaware and Raritan Canal, and mainstem Delaware River where continuous, systematic observations of gage height and discharge are made. These stations are used on a year-round basis in River Master operations.

- **Maximum reservoir depletion.**—The minimum water-surface level or elevation below which a reservoir ceases to continue making delivery of quantities of water for all purposes for which the reservoir was designed. This also is referred to as minimum full-operating level.

- **Rate of flow.**—Mean discharge for a specified 24-hour period, in cubic feet per second or million gallons per day.

- **Rate of flow at Montague.**—Daily mean discharge of the Delaware River at Montague, New Jersey, computed on a calendar-day basis.

- **Reservoir-controlled releases.**—Controlled releases from reservoirs passed through outlet valves in the dams or through turbines in powerplants. These releases do not include spillway overflow at the reservoirs.

- **Storage or contents.**—Usable volume of water in a reservoir. Unless otherwise indicated, volume is computed on the basis of level pool and above the point of maximum depletion.

- **Time of day.**—Time of day is expressed in 24-hour Eastern Standard Time, which during the report year included a 23-hour day on April 2 and a 25-hour day on October 29.

- **Uncontrolled runoff at Montague.**—Runoff from the 3,480 square mile (mi^2) drainage area above Montague, New Jersey, excluding the drainage area above Pepacton, Cannonsville, Neversink, Wallenpaupack, and Rio Dams, but including spillway overflow at these dams.

Precipitation

Precipitation in the Delaware River Basin above Montague, New Jersey, totaled 55.03 in. during the 2006 report year and was 11.36 in. greater than, or 126 percent of, the long-term (65-year) average. Monthly precipitation ranged from 39 percent of the long-term average in March 2006 to 290 percent of average in June 2006. Data on monthly precipitation during the report year and long-term average precipitation are presented in table 1[1]. These data were computed from records collected at 10 geographically distributed stations by the NWS; the New York City Department of Environmental Protection, Bureau of Water Supply; and the River Master office.

---

[1]All numbered tables in the section "Delaware River Operations" are grouped at the end of this section, beginning on page 23.

The seasonal period from December to May typically is when surface-water and groundwater reservoirs refill. During this period in 2005–2006, total precipitation was 19.26 in., which is 95 percent of the 65-year average. During June to November, total precipitation was 35.77 in., which is 153 percent of the long-term average. The maximum monthly precipitation was 11.62 in. in June 2006, measured at Fishs Eddy, New York; the minimum monthly precipitation was 1.32 in. in March 2006, measured at Neversink, New York (locations shown on fig. 1).

Operations

December to May

Operations on December 1, 2005, were conducted as prescribed by the Decree. The Montague flow objective was 1,750 ft^3/s, and the allowable diversions to New York City and New Jersey were 800 Mgal/d and 100 Mgal/d, respectively. Conservation releases from New York City reservoirs were made at the rates shown in table 2, which are incorporated in Delaware River Basin Commission (DRBC) Docket D-77-20 CP (Revision 7).

From December 2005 to May 2006, the first half of the report year, total precipitation was 1.06 in. below average. Monthly precipitation ranged from 39 percent of the long-term average in March 2006 to 172 percent in January 2006 (table 1). Runoff in the upper basin was above normal in January and February, normal in December and May, and below normal in March and April.

On December 1, 2005, when the 2006 report year began, Pepacton Reservoir contained 114.728 Bgal of water in storage above the point of maximum depletion, or 81.8 percent of the 140.190 Bgal storage capacity. Cannonsville Reservoir contained 66.974 Bgal, or 70.0 percent of the 95.706 Bgal storage capacity. Neversink Reservoir contained 31.471 Bgal, or 90.1 percent of the 34.941 Bgal storage capacity. Combined storage in these reservoirs on December 1, 2005, was 213.173 Bgal, or 78.7 percent of combined capacity. Daily storage in Pepacton, Cannonsville, and Neversink Reservoirs is given in tables 3, 4, and 5, respectively, and combined storage during the report year is shown in figure 2.

The Decree Parties continued an experimental augmented conservation releases program for the New York City Delaware Basin Reservoirs that began on May 1, 2004. This program established a habitat protection bank, which consisted of an excess release quantity bank, a thermal protection bank, and a supplemental release bank. It also established flow targets for all three tailwaters at certain USGS gaging stations downstream of the reservoirs.

On February 8, 2006, in consideration of hydrologic conditions resulting in high storage levels in Pepacton and Neversink Reservoirs, the Decree Parties implemented a temporary spill reduction program. This program attempted to manage a storage void to completely capture runoff from a 1-inch rainfall event and to reduce or eliminate spills through the use of preemptive controlled releases. This temporary program ran concurrently with the snowpack-based spill reduction program implemented in 2004. The agreements for the temporary spill reduction program are presented in Appendix A for Pepacton Reservoir and in Appendix B for Neversink Reservoir.

From December to May, inflow to the City's reservoirs typically exceeds outflow and, consequently, storage increases. The average inflow to Pepacton, Cannonsville, and Neversink Reservoirs for this

6-month period, computed on the basis of the 65-year period from December 1940 to May 2005, was 302.3 Bgal. During the corresponding 6 months of the report year, inflow to the three reservoirs totaled 289.7 Bgal. Evaporation loss is not included in the computations.

Combined storage increased steadily from December 2005 to mid-January 2006, when the reservoirs filled. Combined storage remained high during winter, then increased to full capacity in late April. The combined storage of the reservoirs was about 100 percent of capacity on May 31, 2006.

Combined storage in the three New York City reservoirs was 206.391 Bgal on November 30, 2005, and 271.950 Bgal on May 31, 2006, a net increase of 65.559 Bgal or 24.2 percent of total capacity. The maximum combined storage during the December to May period was 281.750 Bgal on January 19, 2006. Maximum storage in Pepacton Reservoir during the December to May period was 144.060 Bgal on January 19; maximum storage in Cannonsville Reservoir was 102.192 Bgal on January 19; and maximum storage in Neversink Reservoir was 35.498 Bgal on January 19, 2006. Pepacton Reservoir spilled from January 15 to February 14, April 24 to May 4, and May 13–31. Cannonsville Reservoir spilled from January 9 to May 31. Neversink Reservoir spilled from January 15 to February 11 and May 14–26. The combined spill volume from the three reservoirs during this period was 138.063 Bgal.

During the December to May period, diversions to Rondout Reservoir by New York City totaled 59.191 Bgal (325 Mgal/d). The forecasted discharge at Montague, exclusive of water released from the City reservoirs, was greater than the flow objective on all days within the period, and no releases were directed. The observed daily mean discharge at Montague was greater than the applicable flow objective on all days. Applicable design rates for the USGS gaging station Delaware River at Montague, New Jersey, are presented in table 6.

June to November

Monthly precipitation for the June to November period was above average in June, September, October, and November and below average in July and August. Total precipitation during the period was 35.77 in. or 12.45 in. more than the 65-year average (table 1).

Combined storage in the three New York City reservoirs was 272.330 Bgal on June 1, 2006, and 270.643 Bgal on November 30, 2006, a net decrease of 1.687 Bgal or about 0.6 percent of total capacity. During the June to November period, maximum storage in Pepacton Reservoir was 145.717 Bgal on June 28; 108.873 Bgal in Cannonsville Reservoir on June 29; and 35.778 Bgal in Neversink Reservoir on June 28. Maximum combined storage in the three reservoirs was 289.426 Bgal on June 29, 2006. The combined spill volume from the three reservoirs during this period was 171.073 Bgal.

Releases were directed to meet the Montague flow objective on 27 days between June 1 and November 30, 2006, when the forecasted discharge at Montague, exclusive of water released from the New York City reservoirs, was less than the flow objective. Releases at rates designed to protect the fishery and aquatic habitat were made at other times during the period.

From June 1 to June 14, the Montague flow objective was 1,750 ft³/s. The forecasted flow, exclusive of releases from Pepacton, Cannonsville, and Neversink Reservoirs, did not fall below the flow objective and no releases were directed.

The New York City Department of Environmental Protection, Bureau of Water Supply, Quality, and Protection furnished the River Master with the following data for the 2006 calendar year, as stipulated by the Decree:

1. The estimated continuous safe yield from all the City's sources, obtainable without pumping, is 1,665 Mgal/d, or a total during calendar year 2006 of 1.665 Bgal/d x 365 days = 607.725 Bgal.

2. The estimated consumption that the City must provide for, from all its sources of supply during calendar year 2006, is 591.582 + 7.250 = 598.832 Bgal.

On the basis of the Decree and the above-noted data, the aggregate quantity of excess-release water was 83 percent of (607.725 - 598.832), or 7.381 Bgal.

Data on water consumption by the City of New York for each calendar year since 1950, from all sources of supply, are presented in table 7.

As part of the reservoir releases program stipulated in DRBC Docket No. D-77-20 CP (Revision No. 7), about 42 percent of the annual excess-release quantity was placed in a habitat protection bank. The remainder of the excess-release quantity could be used to provide an increase in the Montague flow objective or could be banked in accordance with the procedures given in the DRBC's Lower Basin Drought Management Plan.

On June 15, 2006, the beginning of the seasonal excess-release period, the Montague flow objective was increased to 1,800 ft³/s. Storage in the New York City reservoirs declined slowly from July to August, remained steady from September to mid-October, then increased to nearly full or full levels from late October to the end of the report year.

Excessive rainfall of more than 7 in. over a 3-day period in late June 2006 resulted in a major flood in the Delaware River Basin. The USGS Delaware River at Montague, New Jersey streamflow gaging station recorded a peak stage of 32.15 ft on June 29, 2006, corresponding to a discharge of 212,000 ft³/s.

On September 21, 2006, the Decree Parties implemented a new temporary spill mitigation program for Neversink, Pepacton, and Cannonsville Reservoirs. The interim programs for Pepacton and Neversink Reservoirs, effective November 1, 2005, and the rainfall event based temporary spill reduction programs for Pepacton and Neversink Reservoirs, effective February 8, 2006, were suspended for the duration of the new program. The program, DRBC Docket No. D-77-20-CP (Revision 9) expired on May 31, 2007 and is presented in Appendix C.

From June 15 to November 30, 2006, the forecasted flow at Montague, exclusive of releases from the New York City reservoirs, was less than the flow objective on 27 days and releases were directed by the River Master. On 4 days during the June 15 to November 30 period, the observed flow was less than the flow objective. On 3 of these 4 days, observed flows were within 10 percent of the flow objective. Applicable design rates for the USGS gaging station Delaware River at Montague, New Jersey, are presented in table 6.

The total discharge observed at Montague, the portion derived from uncontrolled runoff from the drainage area below the reservoirs, the portion contributed by power reservoirs, and the portion contributed by Pepacton, Cannonsville, and Neversink Reservoirs during August 2006 are shown in figure 3. In developing the water budget for Montague, uncontrolled runoff was computed as the residual of observed flow minus releases and spills from all reservoirs, and, consequently, was subject to errors in observations, transit times, and routing of the various components of flow. The conservation release from Rio Reservoir is included in the uncontrolled runoff component. The net effect of these uncertainties is incorporated in the computation of uncontrolled runoff. From June 1 to November 30, 2006, diversions from the three New York City Delaware Basin reservoirs to Rondout Reservoir totaled 78.900 Bgal.

Summary of Operations

From December 1, 2005 to November 30, 2006, diversions from the three New York City reservoirs in the upper Delaware River Basin to Rondout Reservoir totaled 138.091 Bgal, and all releases from the three reservoirs to the Delaware River totaled 135.791 Bgal. River Master directed releases to the Delaware River from these reservoirs totaled 14.248 Bgal.

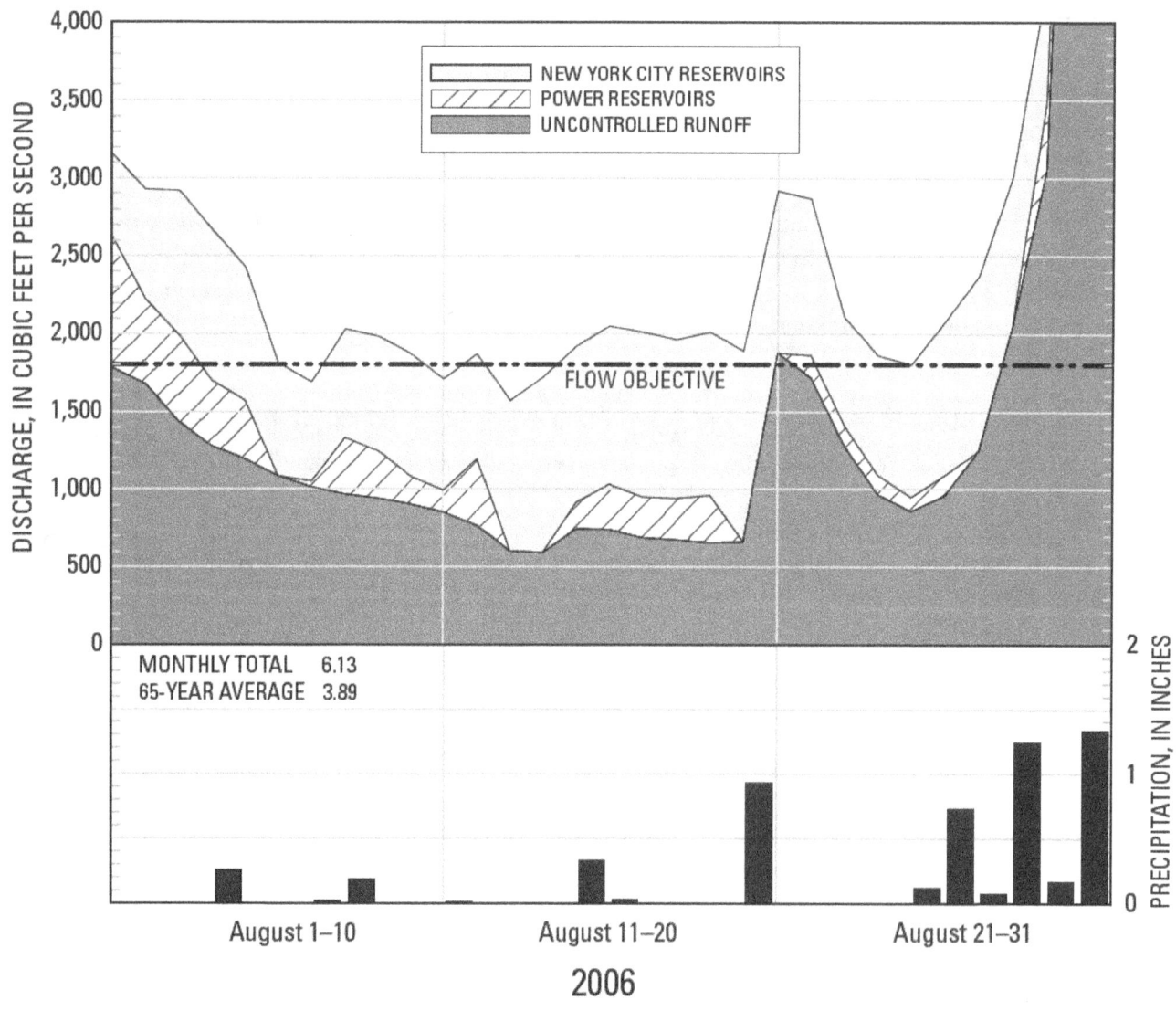

Figure 3. Components of flow, Delaware River at Montague, New Jersey, August 2006.

During the year, maximum storage in Pepacton Reservoir was 145.717 Bgal (103.9 percent of capacity) on June 28, 2006; 108.873 Bgal (113.8 percent of capacity) in Cannonsville Reservoir on June 29; and 35.778 Bgal (102.4 percent of capacity) in Neversink Reservoir on June 28. Maximum combined storage in the three reservoirs was 289.426 Bgal (106.9 percent of combined capacity) on June 29, 2006. The combined spill volume from the three reservoirs for the report year was 309.136 Bgal.

During the report year, minimum storage in Pepacton Reservoir was 114.728 Bgal (81.8 percent of capacity) on December 1, 2005; 66.974 Bgal (70.0 percent of capacity) in Cannonsville Reservoir on December 1, 2005; and 22.709 Bgal (65.0 percent of capacity) in Neversink Reservoir on August 29, 2006. Minimum combined storage in the three reservoirs was 213.173 Bgal (78.7 percent of combined capacity) on December 1, 2005.

On November 30, 2006, the end of the report year, combined storage in the three reservoirs was 270.643 Bgal or 99.9 percent of combined capacity. From December 1, 2005 to November 30, 2006, the net change in combined storage was +57.470 Bgal, or an increase equivalent to 21.2 percent of combined capacity.

Combined storage for the three reservoirs on the first day of the month was above median in all months of the report year (fig. 4). A new record-high combined storage level for the first day of the month was set in February 2006.

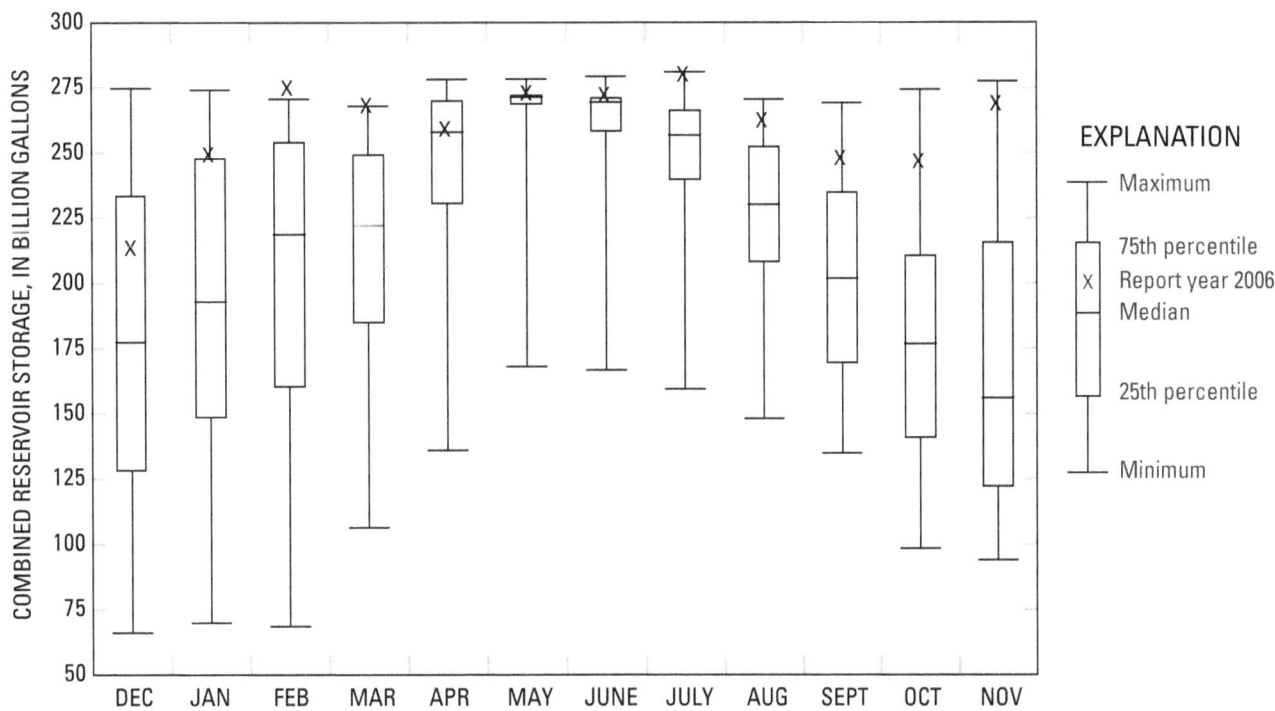

Figure 4. Combined storage in Pepacton, Cannonsville, and Neversink Reservoirs on the first day of the month, December 2005 to November 2006 (this report year), and summary statistics for the reference period, June 1967 to November 2005.

Streamflow

Components of Flow, Delaware River at Montague, New Jersey

The data and computations of the various components of flow form the basic operational records used by the River Master to carry out specific responsibilities related to the Montague formula. The operational record has two parts: forecasted flow at Montague, exclusive of controlled releases from New York City's reservoirs (table 8), and segregation of components of daily mean flow at Montague (table 9).

The following components may be present in the flow of the Delaware River at Montague:

1. Controlled releases from Lake Wallenpaupack on Wallenpaupack Creek, for the production of hydroelectric power.

2. Controlled releases from Rio Reservoir on Mongaup River, for the production of hydroelectric power.

3. Runoff from the uncontrolled area above Montague, including spills from New York City reservoirs, Lake Wallenpaupack, and Rio Reservoir.

4. Controlled releases from Pepacton, Cannonsville, and Neversink Reservoirs of New York City.

The releases from New York City's reservoirs necessary to meet the Montague flow objective were computed on the basis of the forecasted flow at Montague, exclusive of controlled releases from the reservoirs.

Time of Travel

Following are average times for the effective travel of water from the various sources of controlled supply to Montague, New Jersey. These times were used for flow routing during the 2006 report year.

Source	Travel time, in hours
Pepacton Reservoir	60
Cannonsville Reservoir	48
Neversink Reservoir	33
Lake Wallenpaupack	16
Rio Reservoir	8

Travel times were computed from reservoir and powerplant operations data and historical streamflow records. The travel times generally are suitable for use in the operations of the River Master. Occasionally, however, significant exceptions are observed. For example, when a large release from Cannonsville Reservoir follows a small release, a substantial portion of the water fills the channel en route, and the remainder may arrive at Montague as much as 66 hours after the time of release. During winter, the formation of ice, together with lower streamflow, gradually increases the resistance to water flow, resulting in increased travel times. Because ice-affected travel times increase gradually over several days, and releases were not directed to meet the Montague flow objective during periods of ice, no adjustments were made to compensate for increased travel times during these periods of the report year.

Segregation of Flow at Montague

The River Master daily operations record of reservoir releases and segregation of the various components contributing to the flow of the Delaware River at Montague, New Jersey, are presented in table 9. The data are arranged to conform to the downstream movement of water from the various sources to Montague. Summation of data across individual rows in the table is equivalent to routing the various flow contributions to Montague, using the above-noted average travel times. Uncontrolled runoff was computed as a residual by subtracting the flow contributions of all other sources from the observed discharge at Montague.

Computation of Directed Releases

During the report year, the River Master used the following information for daily operations: (1) discharges computed from recorded or reported stream gage heights, for various 24-hour periods, absent real-time information on any changes in stage-discharge relations; (2) daily discharge from New York City's three Delaware Basin reservoirs, measured with venturi meters; (3) precipitation reports for the previous 24 hours; (4) actual powerplant releases converted to daily discharges; (5) advance estimates of power demand converted to daily discharges; (6) advance estimates of uncontrolled runoff at Montague; and (7) average travel times for routing water from various sources. Although uncertainty is inherent in the advance estimates, this information is used by necessity in the daily design and direction of reservoir releases.

The 60-hour travel time of water from Pepacton Reservoir to Montague is greater than the travel time of water from any other reservoir in the upper Delaware River Basin. Releases from Cannonsville and Neversink Reservoirs were timed to arrive at Montague concurrently with releases from Pepacton Reservoir. To allow for differences in travel times, daily directed releases were scheduled to begin from Pepacton Reservoir at 1200 hours, from Cannonsville Reservoir at 2400 hours, and from Neversink Reservoir at 1500 hours the following day.

Releases from the City's reservoirs required to meet the Montague flow objective were computed from forecasts of releases from Lake Wallenpaupack and Rio Reservoir, and estimates of uncontrolled runoff at Montague. To account for the travel times from these sources to Montague, the computation requires estimates of the following components of flow two or more days in advance: (1) release of water from Lake Wallenpaupack; (2) release of water from Rio Reservoir; and (3) uncontrolled runoff from the drainage area upstream of Montague. The River Master operations record for computing daily directed release requirements during periods of low flow is given in table 8.

The electric utilities furnished forecasts of power generation and releases. Because the hydroelectric plants were used chiefly for area regulation or meeting peak power demands, the forecasts were subject to various modifying factors, including the vagaries of weather on electricity demand. In addition, because the power companies are members of regional transmission organizations, demand for power outside of the local service area may unexpectedly affect generation schedules. Consequently, at times, the actual use of water for power generation differs considerably from the forecasts used in the design of reservoir releases.

For computational purposes during periods of low flow, estimates of uncontrolled runoff at Montague were treated as two components: (1) current runoff and (2) forecasted increase in runoff from precipitation. Estimates of these components are given in table 8.

During ice-free conditions, current runoff was computed using a routing and recession procedure based on discharges at 0800 hours at the following USGS gaging stations:

Station Name	Drainage Area (mi^2)
Beaver Kill at Cooks Falls, New York	241
Oquaga Creek at Deposit, New York	67.6
Equinunk Creek at Equinunk, Pennsylvania	56.3
Callicoon Creek at Callicoon, New York	110
Tenmile River at Tusten, New York	45.6
Lackawaxen River at Hawley, Pennsylvania	290
Shohola Creek near Shohola, Pennsylvania	83.6
Neversink River at Port Jervis, New York	336

During winter, the advance estimate of uncontrolled runoff (current conditions) was made on the basis of observed flows at a reduced network of gaging stations and the recession curve for computed uncontrolled flow at Montague.

The forecasted runoff from precipitation is shown in table 8 under the heading "Weather Adjustment." Throughout the year, the NWS office in Binghamton, New York, furnished quantitative forecasts of average precipitation and air temperatures for the 3,480-mi^2 drainage basin upstream of Montague, New Jersey. During winter, runoff was estimated on the basis of the current status of snow and ice, along with forecasted precipitation and temperature. During other periods, forecasted precipitation was used to estimate runoff.

The forecasted flow at Montague, exclusive of releases from New York City's Delaware Basin reservoirs (table 8), is computed as the sum of forecasted releases from power reservoirs, estimated uncontrolled runoff including conservation releases from Rio Reservoir, and weather adjustments. If the computed total flow is less than the flow objective at Montague, then the deficiency is made up by releases from the City's reservoirs, as directed by the River Master.

When forecasts of precipitation or powerplant releases were revised appreciably after a release was directed, the release required from the City's reservoirs was recomputed. Commonly, this procedure resulted in a reduced release requirement for New York City reservoirs for that day. Only final figures for releases from New York City reservoirs are given in table 8.

Analysis of Forecasts

Forecasts of streamflow at Montague, developed on the basis of anticipated contributions from the components described previously but excluding releases from New York City's reservoirs, differed on most days from observed flow. Occasionally, variations in the components were partially compensating and observed flows compared favorably with forecasted flows.

On any given day, forecasted releases and actual releases can differ considerably. The ranges of actual daily releases from August 6 to August 30, 2006, are as follows: daily releases at Lake Wallenpaupack differed from forecasted releases by 44 ft³/s less to 835 ft³/s more, and daily releases at Rio Reservoir differed from forecasted releases by 152 ft³/s less to 121 ft³/s more. On the basis of observed flows at Montague, total directed releases from New York City's Delaware Basin reservoirs during the report year were about 38 percent more than required for exact forecasting.

Comparison of hydrographs of forecasted daily runoff and observed daily runoff from the uncontrolled area (fig. 5) indicates that the forecasts generally were suitable for use in designing releases from New York City's Delaware Basin reservoirs. Numerical adjustments to the designs were made when needed to compensate for errors in the forecasts, but, because of travel times, the effects of the adjustments on flows at Montague were not evident until several days after the design date.

Analysis of the precipitation forecasts shows that the total precipitation amount forecasted for the 3-day design periods is reasonably accurate, but often the actual timing of precipitation events may be

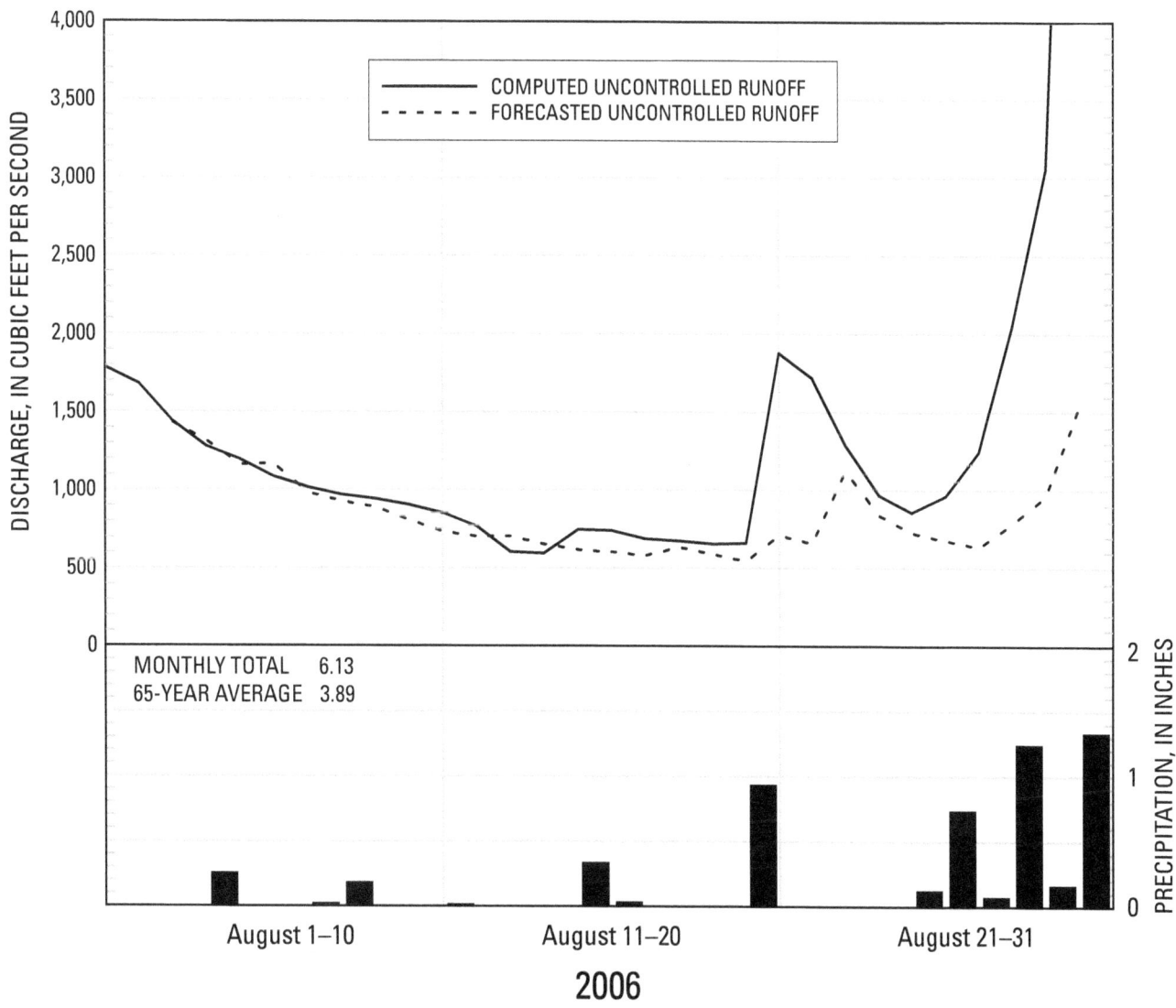

Figure 5. Uncontrolled runoff component, Delaware River at Montague, New Jersey, August 2006.

earlier or later than forecasted. The accuracy of the runoff forecasts is affected greatly by the timing of precipitation events. In addition, if the actual storm track differs from the forecasted track, the amount and timing of runoff can be substantially different than predicted.

Diversions to New York City Water Supply

The 1954 Amended Decree authorizes New York City to divert water from the Delaware River Basin at a rate not to exceed the equivalent of 800 Mgal/d. The Decree specifies that the diversion rate shall be computed as the aggregate total diversion beginning June 1 of each year divided by the number of days elapsed since the preceding May 31.

Daily diversions during the report year from Pepacton, Cannonsville, and Neversink Reservoirs to the New York City water-supply system (Rondout Reservoir) are given in table 10. A running account of the average rates of combined diversions from the three reservoirs, computed as stipulated by the Decree, also is shown. The following tabulation shows allowable maximum diversion rates and average actual diversions for various periods during the report year.

Effective dates	Allowable diversion (Mgal/d)	Average actual diversion (Mgal/d)
December 1, 2005 to May 31, 2006	800	464
June 1 to November 30, 2006	800	431

During the report year, a total of 138.091 Bgal of water was diverted to the New York City water-supply system. The allowable diversion was 328.108 Bgal.

Storage in New York City Reservoirs

The following tabulation summarizes the "point of maximum depletion" and other pertinent levels and contents of Pepacton, Cannonsville, and Neversink Reservoirs. This information was provided by the New York City Board of Water Supply.

Level	Pepacton Reservoir		Cannonsville Reservoir		Neversink Reservoir	
	Elevation (ft)	Contents (Bgal)	Elevation (ft)	Contents (Bgal)	Elevation (ft)	Contents (Bgal)
Full pool or spillway crest	1,280.00	*140.190	1,150.00	*95.706	1,440.00	*34.941
Point of maximum depletion	1,152.00	*3.511	1,040.00	*1.020	1,319.00	*0.525
Sill of diversion tunnel	1,143.00	*4.200	+1,035.00	*1.564	1,314.00	
Sill of river outlet tunnel	1,126.50		1,020.50		1,314.00	
Dead storage		1.800		0.328		1.680

*Contents shown are quantities stored between listed elevations.

+Elevation of mouth of inlet channel of diversion works.

Daily storage in Pepacton, Cannonsville, and Neversink Reservoirs, above the "point of maximum depletion" or minimum full-operating level, is given in tables 3, 4, and 5.

On December 1, 2005, combined storage in the three reservoirs was 213.173 Bgal, or 78.7 percent of combined capacity. Combined storage increased in early winter and remained at high levels throughout the year. Storage during the report year did not decline below 78 percent of total capacity. The three reservoirs spilled a total of 309.136 Bgal during the year. Combined storage reached a maximum for the report year on June 29, 2006, at 289.426 Bgal. Combined storage was 270.643 Bgal, or 99.9 percent of combined capacity, on November 30, 2006.

Comparison of River Master Operations Data With Other Streamflow Records

River Master operations are conducted on a day-to-day basis and, by necessity, use preliminary data on streamflow. In this section, records used in River Master operations are compared to final data published for selected USGS gaging stations. Data on releases were reported in million gallons per day and converted to cubic feet per second for use in the comparisons.

Releases from New York City Reservoirs

River Master operations data on controlled releases from Pepacton, Cannonsville, and Neversink Reservoirs to the Delaware River were furnished by the New York City Department of Environmental Protection. These data were obtained from calibrated instruments connected to venturi meters installed in the outlet conduits of the reservoirs.

The USGS gaging station on East Branch Delaware River at Downsville, New York, is 0.5 mile downstream from Downsville Dam (fig. 1). Discharge measured at this station includes releases from Pepacton Reservoir and a small amount of seepage and any runoff that enters the channel between the dam and the gaging station. The drainage area is 371 mi^2 at the dam and 372 mi^2 at the gaging station.

The following tabulation compares releases from Pepacton Reservoir (table 9), reported by New York City, to the final records for the USGS gaging station on East Branch Delaware River at Downsville, New York (table 11), for the flow objectives shown.

Flow objective (ft^3/s)	12	36	85	186	699
Number of USGS daily mean discharge values used in comparison	11	26	8	14	13
New York City-measured mean flow (ft^3/s)	12.4	35.6	85.1	186	699
USGS-computed mean flow (ft^3/s)	16.1	41.8	80.0	172	705
Percent difference	-23.0	-14.8	+6.4	+8.1	-0.9

The differences at the four higher flow objectives are less than 15 percent. The instruments connected to the venturi meters were recalibrated periodically by New York City to improve the accuracy of the recorded flow data.

The USGS gaging station on West Branch Delaware River at Stilesville, New York, is 1.4 miles downstream from Cannonsville Dam (fig. 1). Discharge measured at this station includes releases from Cannonsville Reservoir and runoff from 2 mi^2 of drainage area between the dam and the gaging station. The drainage area is 454 mi^2 at the dam and 456 mi^2 at the gaging station. The gaging-station records are rated fair at flows greater than 100 ft³/s and poor at flows less than 100 ft³/s. A rating of "fair" means that about 95 percent of the daily discharges are within 15 percent of the true discharge, whereas a rating of "poor" means that daily discharges have less than "fair" accuracy. The records include runoff from the area between the dam and the gaging station, and seepage near the base of the dam.

The following tabulation compares releases from Cannonsville Reservoir (table 9), reported by New York City, to the final records for the USGS gaging station on West Branch Delaware River at Stilesville, New York (table 12), for the flow objectives shown.

Flow objective (ft³/s)	46	1,000
Number of USGS daily mean discharge values used in comparison	19	27
New York City-measured mean flow (ft³/s)	46.4	1,000
USGS-computed mean flow (ft³/s)	54.8	1,020
Percent difference	-15.3	-2.0

The USGS gaging station on Neversink River at Neversink, New York, is 1,650 ft downstream from Neversink Dam (fig. 1). Discharge measured at this station includes releases from Neversink Reservoir and, during storms, a small amount of runoff that originates between the dam and the gaging station. The drainage area is 92.5 mi² at the dam and 92.6 mi² at the gaging station.

The following tabulation compares releases from Neversink Reservoir (table 9), reported by New York City, to the final records for the USGS gaging station on Neversink River at Neversink, New York (table 13), for the flow objectives shown.

Flow objective (ft³/s)	25	65	108	190
Number of USGS daily mean discharge values used in comparison	49	23	6	21
New York City-measured mean flow (ft³/s)	24.8	65.0	108	191
USGS-computed mean flow (ft³/s)	26.8	64.0	112	183
Percent difference	-7.5	+1.6	-3.6	+4.4

The differences at the four flow objectives are less than 8 percent. The comparison excludes data for the period from February 20 to June 6, 2006. During this period, the two records differ significantly, with greater flow indicated by the USGS gaging station record. The USGS record was estimated during this period and was downgraded because of heavy debris accumulations on the artificial control.

Delaware River at Montague, New Jersey

The River Master's operations record for the Delaware River at Montague, New Jersey (table 9), showed about 0.1 percent less discharge for the report year than the published USGS record for the gaging station (table 14). Daily values for the two records agreed closely, except during ice-affected periods.

Diversion Tunnels

Records of diversions through the East Delaware, West Delaware, and Neversink Tunnels (fig. 1) were furnished by the New York City Department of Environmental Protection. These records were obtained from the City's calibrated instruments connected to venturi meters installed in the tunnel conduits. The measured flows were transmitted electronically on a 15-second interval to a City computer and, on 5-minute intervals, release and diversion quantities for the preceding 5-minute period were computed using the instantaneous rate-of-flow data from each instrument. These 5-minute quantities were then summed to compute daily total flows, which were reported to the River Master's office on a daily basis. On a weekly basis, the diversion figures were checked against the flow meter totalizer readings and corrected when necessary.

The East Delaware Tunnel is used to divert water from Pepacton Reservoir to Rondout Reservoir. Conditions in the outlet channel of the East Delaware Tunnel were unfavorable for flow measurements during the report year because of high water levels in Rondout Reservoir.

The generating plant at the downstream end of the East Delaware Tunnel operated most days of the report year. When the powerplant was not in operation, some water leaked through the wicket gates and was not recorded on the totalizer. A current-meter measurement made in 1989 shows that the (assumed constant) rate of leakage is about 8.0 Mgal/d. Because the powerplant was not in operation for the equivalent of 180 days during the 2006 report year, the estimated quantity of unmeasured leakage was about 1.4 Bgal.

The West Delaware Tunnel is used to divert water from Cannonsville Reservoir to Rondout Reservoir. Inspections of the channel below the outlet, when valves were closed, revealed only negligible leakage. A hydroelectric powerplant uses water diverted through the West Delaware Tunnel, but the plant operates only when diversions are less than 300 Mgal/d. When the powerplant is not operating, the valves on the pipelines to the plant are closed, and there is no leakage through the system.

The Neversink Tunnel is used to divert water from Neversink Reservoir to Rondout Reservoir. A hydroelectric powerplant uses water diverted through the Neversink Tunnel. When the powerplant is not operating and the main valve on the diversion tunnel is open, leakage develops that is not recorded on the venturi instruments. One current-meter measurement made in 1999 showed a leakage rate of 16.2 ft^3/s (10.5 Mgal/d). When the powerplant is operating, the leakage is included in the recorded flow. No leakage occurs when the main valve on the tunnel is closed. During the 2006 report year, the powerplant operated part of the day on most days and was not operated the equivalent of 236 days. Using the leakage rate noted above and records of powerplant operation, about 2.5 Bgal of water was diverted but not recorded.

Diversions by New Jersey

The Amended Decree authorizes New Jersey to divert water from the Delaware River and its tributaries in New Jersey, to areas outside of the Delaware River Basin, without compensating releases. These diversions may not exceed 100 Mgal/d as a monthly average, and the daily mean diversion may not exceed 120 Mgal/d. The USGS gaging station on Delaware and Raritan Canal at Port Mercer, New Jersey (fig. 1), is used as the official control point for measuring diversions by New Jersey (table 15).

The following tabulation shows the allowable diversion by New Jersey, the period it was in effect, and the maximum monthly diversion during the report year.

Effective dates	Allowable monthly average diversion (Mgal/d)	Maximum monthly average diversion (Mgal/d)	Month of maximum average diversion
Dec. 1, 2005 to Nov. 30, 2006	100	98.8	July

The maximum daily mean diversion was 110 Mgal on December 15, 2005. Diversions by New Jersey did not exceed the limits stipulated by the Decree.

Conformance of Operations Under the Amended Decree of the U.S. Supreme Court Entered June 7, 1954

From December 1, 2005 to November 30, 2006, operations of the Delaware River Master were conducted as stipulated by the Decree.

Diversions from the Delaware River Basin to the New York City water-supply system did not exceed those authorized by the Decree. Under compensating releases of the Montague Formula, New York City released water from its reservoirs at rates designed by the River Master to meet the applicable flow objectives at Montague, New Jersey. During the report year, New York City complied fully with all directives and requests of the River Master.

Diversions from the Delaware River Basin by New Jersey were within limits stipulated by the Decree. New Jersey complied fully with all directives and requests of the River Master.

Table 1. Precipitation in the Delaware River Basin above Montague, New Jersey.
(Source: National Weather Service, New York City Department of Environmental Protection, and Office of the Delaware River Master)

[All values, except percentages, in inches]

| Month | December 1940 to November 2005 Monthly Average | December 2005 to November 2006 | | | |
| | | Amount | Percent of average | Excess (+) or deficit (-) | |
				Month	Cumulative
December	3.41	2.96	87	-.45	-.45
January	3.02	5.19	172	+2.17	+1.72
February	2.61	1.56	60	-1.05	+.67
March	3.36	1.32	39	-2.04	-1.37
April	3.76	3.80	101	+.04	-1.33
May	4.18	4.43	106	+.25	-1.08
June	4.00	11.62	290	+7.62	+6.54
July	4.06	3.12	77	-.94	+5.60
August	3.89	6.13	158	+2.24	+7.84
September	4.04	5.04	125	+1.00	+8.84
October	3.54	5.16	146	+1.62	+10.46
November	3.80	4.70	124	+.90	+11.36
12 months	43.67	55.03	126		

Table 2. Conservation release rates for New York City reservoirs in the Delaware River Basin.
(Source: DRBC Docket No. D-77-20 CP (Revision 7)

[All values in cubic feet per second]

| Reservoir | Effective dates | Conservation release rates | | | |
		Normal	Watch	Warning	Drought
Pepacton	December 1 to November 30	35	30	25	19
Cannonsville	December 1 to May 31	45	38	32	23
	June 1 to August 31	60	51	43	23
	September 1 to November 30	45	38	32	23
Neversink	December 1 to November 30	25	21	18	15

Table 3. Storage in Pepacton Reservoir, New York, for year ending November 30, 2006.
(River Master daily operations record; gage reading at 0800 hours)

[Storage in millions of gallons above elevation 1,152.00 ft. Add 7,711 million gallons for total contents above sill of outlet tunnel, elevation 1,126.50 ft. Storage at spillway level is 140,190 million gallons]

DAY	DEC	JAN	FEB	MAR	APR	MAY	JUNE	JULY	AUG	SEPT	OCT	NOV
1	114,728	125,331	140,968	137,583	133,725	140,838	140,672	142,435	134,210	128,286	124,949	135,873
2	116,093	126,255	140,875	137,182	133,635	140,764	140,950	141,913	133,815	128,585	125,279	136,399
3	117,357	127,146	140,913	136,781	133,527	140,579	141,098	141,635	133,437	128,708	125,418	136,945
4	118,304	127,987	141,319	136,363	133,437	140,338	141,116	141,375	133,060	128,725	125,488	137,236
5	119,121	128,409	141,616	135,928	133,455	140,098	141,042	141,319	132,683	128,637	125,540	137,401
6	119,784	129,077	141,839	135,475	133,815	139,951	140,931	141,098	132,218	128,620	125,557	137,601
7	120,395	129,642	141,764	135,511	134,246	139,896	140,783	141,005	131,755	128,514	125,453	137,657
8	120,480	130,067	141,653	135,566	134,444	139,822	140,875	140,709	131,273	128,339	125,314	137,638
9	121,294	130,475	141,412	135,620	134,570	139,693	141,301	140,486	130,777	128,093	125,157	138,498
10	121,626	130,883	141,061	135,710	134,696	139,565	141,486	140,375	130,280	127,811	124,915	139,050
11	121,951	131,291	140,838	135,801	135,022	139,400	141,653	140,172	129,766	127,495	124,690	139,528
12	122,309	131,969	140,672	135,892	135,185	139,675	141,598	140,080	129,218	127,163	124,412	139,917
13	122,689	133,168	140,560	136,036	135,493	140,061	141,449	139,951	128,655	126,796	124,378	140,209
14	122,791	134,408	140,412	136,073	135,674	140,338	141,245	139,767	128,110	126,394	124,274	140,357
15	122,808	138,022	140,153	136,181	135,910	140,505	141,431	139,528	127,565	126,604	124,153	140,486
16	123,067	140,227	140,024	136,272	136,145	140,634	141,375	139,197	127,023	126,813	123,997	140,486
17	122,981	141,486	139,896	136,272	136,181	140,987	140,857	138,885	126,499	126,831	123,859	141,616
18	122,756	141,969	139,748	136,272	136,199	140,894	140,579	138,535	125,975	126,761	124,101	141,746
19	122,498	144,060	139,932	136,199	136,272	140,931	140,412	138,113	125,401	126,586	124,274	141,598
20	122,258	143,013	139,951	136,127	136,345	140,968	140,375	137,583	126,360	126,516	124,811	141,301
21	122,002	142,416	139,988	135,892	136,345	140,968	140,301	137,090	126,709	126,342	126,290	141,024
22	121,557	142,043	140,006	135,747	136,327	141,061	140,098	136,708	126,604	126,115	127,250	140,857
23	121,248	141,839	139,896	135,566	136,908	141,042	139,988	136,526	126,360	125,800	128,040	140,746
24	120,949	141,690	139,601	135,403	139,142	140,987	140,214	136,145	126,028	125,574	128,708	140,875
25	120,605	141,449	139,308	135,185	140,523	140,950	140,505	135,692	125,679	125,331	129,201	140,765
26	120,497	141,098	139,013	135,004	141,024	140,913	141,042	135,222	125,418	124,984	129,731	140,653
27	121,265	140,875	138,664	134,895	141,079	140,950	143,873	134,823	125,174	124,690	130,103	140,560
28	121,488	140,616	138,058	134,588	141,227	140,672	145,717	134,300	125,157	124,291	130,670	140,486
29	121,540	140,505		134,390	141,264	140,431	145,039	134,624	125,019	124,516	133,240	140,634
30	122,670	140,505		134,120	140,931	140,172	143,346	134,534	126,971	124,828	134,931	140,746
31	124,135	140,616		133,959		140,301		134,426	127,829		135,312	
Change	+12,098	+16,481	-2,558	-4,099	+6,972	-630	+3,045	-8,920	-6,597	-3,001	+10,484	+5,434
Equiv. Mgal/d	+390.3	+531.6	-91.4	-132.2	+232.4	-20.3	+101.5	-287.7	-212.8	-100.0	+338.2	+181.1
Equiv. ft³/s	+604	+822	-141	-205	+360	-31.4	+157	-445	-329	-155	+523	+280

Change for year +28,709 Mgal Equivalent for year +78.7 Mgal/d Equivalent for year +122 ft³/s

24

Table 4. Storage in Cannonsville Reservoir, New York, for year ending November 30, 2006.
(River Master daily operations record; gage reading at 0800 hours)

[Storage in millions of gallons above elevation 1,040,00 ft. Add 2,584 million gallons for total contents above sill outlet tunnel, elevation 1,020,50 ft. Storage at spillway level is 95,706 million gallons]

DAY	DEC	JAN	FEB	MAR	APR	MAY	JUNE	JULY	AUG	SEPT	OCT	NOV
1	66,974	88,876	98,474	96,752	96,269	98,040	96,880	101,999	96,623	96,591	95,204	98,410
2	69,080	90,123	98,474	96,703	96,414	97,878	96,816	100,405	96,398	96,977	95,539	98,313
3	70,642	91,264	98,523	96,703	96,447	97,798	96,880	99,521	96,092	97,073	95,819	98,233
4	71,821	92,314	99,038	96,671	96,382	97,540	97,299	98,555	95,964	97,106	95,851	97,959
5	72,788	93,105	99,263	96,671	96,447	97,235	97,476	97,991	95,931	97,122	95,867	97,540
6	73,609	93,866	99,376	96,687	96,463	96,961	97,476	97,573	95,851	97,090	95,867	97,170
7	74,326	94,519	99,183	96,703	96,495	96,735	97,331	97,283	95,706	97,073	95,819	96,848
8	75,044	95,113	98,925	96,607	96,687	96,527	97,235	97,009	95,569	96,945	95,676	96,591
9	75,611	95,660	98,651	96,302	96,735	96,479	97,492	96,784	95,356	96,864	95,478	96,703
10	76,108	96,109	98,426	96,044	96,752	96,623	97,685	96,543	95,220	96,768	95,250	96,832
11	76,550	96,591	98,233	95,948	96,768	96,607	97,862	96,495	95,037	96,703	94,946	96,784
12	76,992	97,057	98,007	95,899	96,752	96,752	97,878	96,527	94,702	96,623	94,747	96,704
13	77,393	97,927	97,878	98,754	96,703	96,880	97,766	96,848	94,276	96,479	94,717	96,655
14	77,655	98,394	97,734	96,205	96,687	96,929	97,589	96,945	93,927	96,463	94,367	96,607
15	77,862	100,276	97,621	97,395	96,768	96,913	97,573	96,848	93,577	96,816	94,018	96,559
16	78,263	100,373	97,540	97,830	96,880	96,880	97,460	96,655	93,212	97,235	93,637	96,414
17	78,761	99,858	97,476	97,975	96,816	96,896	97,122	96,463	92,892	97,283	93,301	99,247
18	79,244	99,553	97,460	97,927	96,719	96,929	96,816	96,141	92,466	97,267	92,755	100,083
19	79,521	102,192	97,347	97,830	96,495	96,961	96,495	95,786	91,979	97,218	92,192	99,826
20	79,673	101,677	97,251	97,750	96,237	97,057	96,575	95,722	92,466	97,073	91,766	99,360
21	79,797	100,743	97,202	97,508	96,141	97,073	96,431	95,676	92,892	96,977	92,451	98,941
22	80,004	99,971	97,186	97,283	96,109	97,186	96,221	95,676	93,029	96,896	92,938	98,603
23	80,156	99,408	97,073	97,170	96,655	97,251	96,205	96,028	92,968	96,527	93,166	98,345
24	80,363	98,973	97,041	97,009	98,700	97,267	96,221	96,173	92,755	96,092	93,501	98,265
25	80,570	98,700	97,009	96,913	99,633	97,186	96,221	96,189	92,177	95,835	93,592	97,959
26	81,148	98,442	96,929	96,832	99,633	97,170	96,736	96,092	91,903	95,448	93,683	97,492
27	82,189	98,233	96,848	96,800	99,311	97,154	99,183	96,060	91,721	95,006	93,729	97,170
28	83,028	97,991	96,784	96,671	98,957	97,138	107,541	96,044	92,055	94,626	93,942	96,800
29	83,663	97,846		96,463	98,603	97,073	108,873	96,382	92,497	94,611	97,186	96,591
30	85,325	97,814		96,414	98,313	96,977	106,023	96,623	94,474	95,022	98,378	96,398
31	87,378	97,959		96,302		96,880		96,719	95,835		98,474	
Change	+23,511	+10,581	-1,175	-482	+2,011	-1,433	+9,143	-9,304	-884	-813	+3,452	-2,076
Equiv. Mgal/d	+758.4	+341.3	-42.0	-15.5	+67.0	-46.2	+304.8	-300.1	-28.5	-27.1	+111.4	-69.2
Equiv. ft³/s	+1,173	+528	-64.9	-24.1	+104	-71.5	+471	-464	-44.1	-41.9	+172	-107

Change for year +32,531 Mgal   Change for year +89.1 Mgal/d   Equivalent for year +138 ft³/s

Table 5. Storage in Neversink Reservoir, New York, for year ending November 30, 2006. (River Master daily operations record; gage reading at 0800 hours)

[Storage in millions of gallons above elevation 1,319.00 ft. Add 525 million gallons for total contents above sill of outlet tunnel, elevation 1,314.00 ft. Storage at spillway level is 34,941 million gallons]

DAY	DEC	JAN	FEB	MAR	APR	MAY	JUNE	JULY	AUG	SEPT	OCT	NOV
1	31,471	33,461	35,066	33,211	28,255	32,824	34,778	35,204	31,550	23,175	26,719	34,253
2	31,911	33,369	35,021	33,115	28,324	32,924	34,705	35,155	31,327	23,266	26,923	34,170
3	32,225	33,317	35,031	33,105	28,394	32,957	34,655	34,951	31,131	23,401	26,979	34,101
4	32,465	33,221	35,204	32,919	28,499	33,038	34,670	34,931	30,845	23,541	27,090	33,959
5	32,647	33,101	35,264	32,639	28,628	33,144	34,650	34,907	30,547	23,721	27,202	33,799
6	32,829	32,981	35,239	32,377	28,751	33,221	34,576	34,700	30,259	23,817	27,292	33,611
7	32,986	32,834	35,169	32,108	28,844	33,264	34,557	34,463	29,923	23,906	27,369	33,432
8	33,115	32,690	35,140	31,832	28,972	33,283	34,670	34,209	29,585	23,991	27,434	33,221
9	33,046	32,533	35,120	31,555	29,088	33,302	34,833	33,988	29,244	24,051	27,494	33,562
10	32,924	32,382	34,917	31,285	29,186	33,317	34,961	33,755	28,839	24,092	27,550	33,674
11	32,781	32,236	34,991	30,984	29,271	33,336	34,981	33,669	28,495	24,076	27,584	33,596
12	32,638	32,481	34,863	30,616	29,347	33,513	34,951	33,591	28,158	24,047	27,670	33,713
13	32,494	32,805	34,665	30,232	29,415	34,463	34,818	33,538	27,805	24,051	27,826	33,813
14	32,302	33,105	34,710	29,932	29,496	34,783	34,778	33,451	27,447	24,043	27,914	33,925
15	32,122	34,586	34,724	29,697	29,598	35,001	34,823	33,297	27,116	24,871	27,983	34,037
16	31,986	35,041	34,739	29,428	29,702	35,001	34,808	33,153	26,774	25,483	28,058	34,135
17	32,118	35,140	34,586	29,101	29,778	35,155	34,744	32,995	26,435	25,762	28,114	35,061
18	32,232	35,199	34,379	28,747	29,846	35,115	34,660	32,834	26,076	25,959	28,539	35,269
19	32,316	35,498	34,086	28,403	29,914	35,090	34,562	32,634	25,725	26,118	28,897	35,229
20	32,391	35,264	33,775	28,058	29,977	35,120	34,463	32,615	25,475	26,261	29,258	35,194
21	32,444	35,199	33,489	27,988	30,050	35,075	34,507	32,491	25,197	26,363	30,060	35,150
22	32,458	35,165	33,523	28,027	30,114	35,056	34,517	32,411	24,858	26,465	30,461	35,100
23	32,500	35,165	33,610	28,027	30,337	35,026	34,453	32,477	24,507	26,545	30,744	34,941
24	32,542	35,160	33,698	28,045	31,290	35,011	34,405	32,420	24,153	26,642	30,952	34,798
25	32,580	35,110	33,751	28,088	31,785	35,001	34,355	32,339	23,777	26,723	31,136	34,601
26	32,733	35,056	33,803	28,119	32,080	34,961	34,705	32,245	23,465	26,732	31,294	34,414
27	32,919	34,976	33,838	28,167	32,292	34,877	35,613	32,151	23,155	26,697	31,424	34,189
28	33,048	34,946	33,654	28,185	32,458	34,892	35,778	32,000	22,921	26,710	31,681	33,964
29	33,115	34,941		28,211	32,596	34,863	35,514	31,761	22,709	26,701	31,543	33,731
30	33,446	34,986		28,202	32,709	34,818	35,289	31,639	22,957	26,697	34,032	33,499
31	33,499	35,036		28,224		34,769			23,072		34,287	
Change	+3,012	+1,537	-1,382	-5,430	+4,485	+2,060	+520	-3,650	-8,567	+3,625	+7,590	-788
Equiv. Mgal/d	+97.2	+49.6	-49.4	-175.2	+149.5	+66.5	+17.3	-117.7	-276.4	+120.8	+244.8	-26.3
Equiv. ft³/s	+150	+76.7	-76.4	-271	+231	+103	+26.8	-182	-428	+187	+379	-40.6

Change for year +3,012 Mgal

Equivalent for year +8.25 Mgal/d

Equivalent for year +12.8 ft³/s

Table 6. Design rates for Delaware River at Montague, New Jersey, gaging station, December 1, 2005 to November 30, 2006. (Source: Office of the Delaware River Master)

[Rates in cubic feet per second]

Effective dates	Montague Design Rate
December 1 to December 18, 2005	1,750
December 19, 2005 to March 15, 2006	1,800
March 16 to June 14, 2006	1,750
June 15 to August 31, 2006	1,800
September 1 to November 30, 2006	1,750

Table 7. Consumption of water by New York City, 1950 to 2006.
(Source: New York City Department of Environmental Protection, Bureau of Water Supply)

[Mgal/d, million gallons per day; Bgal, billion gallons]

Year	Average daily consumption			Annual Consumption (Bgal)
	City Proper (Mgal/d)	Outside Communities (Mgal/d)	Total (Mgal/d)	
1950	953.3	29.1	982.4	358.576
51	1,041.9	28.1	1,070.0	390.550
52	1,087.0	32.7	1,119.7	409.810
53	1,093.9	44.6	1,138.5	415.552
54	1,063.4	46.3	1,109.7	405.040
1955	1,109.9	45.3	1,155.2	421.648
56	1,111.3	48.9	1,160.2	424.633
57	1,169.0	57.2	1,226.2	447.563
58	1,152.9	49.6	1,202.5	438.912
59	1,204.3	60.3	1,264.6	461.579
1960	1,199.4	58.9	1,258.3	460.529
61	1,221.0	64.0	1,285.0	469.022
62	1,207.6	68.8	1,276.4	465.896
63	1,218.0	76.7	1,294.7	472.582
64	1,189.2	79.4	1,268.6	464.295
1965	1,052.1	71.2	1,123.3	409.995
66	1,044.9	73.2	1,118.1	408.128
67	1,135.3	71.0	1,206.3	440.302
68	1,242.0	78.2	1,320.2	483.175
69	1,328.7	80.1	1,408.8	514.229
1970	1,400.3	90.4	1,490.7	544.116
71	1,423.6	87.9	1,511.5	551.695
72	1,412.4	83.0	1,495.4	547.340
73	1,448.9	95.4	1,544.3	563.681
74	1,441.8	96.3	1,538.1	561.409
1975	1,415.0	92.1	1,507.1	550.093
76	1,435.0	95.8	1,530.8	560.264
77	1,483.0	104.7	1,587.7	579.510
78	1,479.4	103.0	1,582.4	577.566
79	1,513.0	104.6	1,617.6	590.426
1980	1,506.3	110.1	1,616.3	591.582
81	1,309.5	100.0	1,409.5	514.475
82	1,383.0	104.8	1,487.8	543.060
83	1,424.2	112.6	1,536.8	561.010
84	1,465.2	113.9	1,579.1	577.963
1985	1,325.4	106.5	1,431.9	522.656
86	1,351.1	115.2	1,466.3	535.200
87	1,447.1	119.8	1,566.9	571.885
88	1,484.3	125.6	1,609.9	589.090
89	1,402.0	113.4	1,515.4	553.158
1990	1,424.4	122.4	1,546.8	564.577
91	1,469.9	123.6	1,593.5	581.628
92	1,368.7	113.9	1,482.6	542.632
93	1,368.9	118.8	1,487.7	543.011
94	1,357.8	119.2	1,477.0	539.105
1995	1,326.1	123.1	1,449.2	528.958
96	1,283.5	120.2	1,403.7	512.351
97	1,201.3	123.5	1,324.8	483.552
98	1,220.0	124.7	1,344.7	490.816
99	1,237.2	128.6	1,365.8	498.517

Table 7. Consumption of water by New York City, 1950 to 2006.—Continued
(Source: New York City Department of Environmental Protection, Bureau of Water Supply)

[Mgal/d, million gallons per day; Bgal, billion gallons]

| Year | Average daily consumption | | | Annual Consumption (Bgal) |
	City Proper (Mgal/d)	Outside Communities (Mgal/d)	Total (Mgal/d)	
2000	1,240.4	124.9	1,365.3	499.700
01	1,184.0	128.4	1,312.4	479.026
02	1,135.6	121.1	1,256.7	458.696
03	1,093.7	115.9	1,209.6	441.516
04	1,099.6	117.5	1,217.1	445.461
2005	1,107.6	123.8	1,231.4	449.462
06	1,069.2	116.8	1,186.0	432.890

Table 8. New York City reservoir release design data.
(River Master daily operation record)

[ft³/s, cubic feet per second; (ft³/s)-d, cubic feet per second days; Col., Column]

Date of advance estimate	Advance estimate of discharge of Delaware River at Montague, New Jersey, exclusive of New York City reservoir releases									Computation of balancing adjustment					
	Powerplant release forecasts		Uncontrolled runoff		Montague date	Discharge (ft³/s)	Indicated deficiency	Balancing adjustment (ft³/s)	Directed release (ft³/s)	Adjusted directed release		Actual deficiency		Cumulative difference (ft³/s)-d	Balancing adjustment (ft³/s)
	Lake Wallenpaupack (ft³/s)	Rio Reservoir (ft³/s)	Current condition (ft³/s)	Weather adjustment (ft³/s)						Daily (ft³/s)	Cumulative (ft³/s)-d	Daily (ft³/s)	Cumulative (ft³/s)-d		
2006	Col. 1	Col. 2	Col. 3	Col. 4	2006	Col. 5	Col. 6	Col. 7	Col. 8	Col. 9	Col. 10	Col. 11	Col. 12	Col. 13	Col. 14
July 27	0	152	1,112	255	July 30	1,519	281	0	281	281	281	0	0	281	-28
28	106	89	1,114	111	31	1,420	380	0	380	380	661	0	0	661	-50
July 29	292	152	1,428	58	Aug. 1	1,930	0	0	0	0	661	0	0	661	-50
30	292	152	1,359	5	2	1,808	0	0	0	0	661	0	0	661	-50
31	292	152	1,418	11	3	1,873	0	-28	0	0	661	0	0	661	-50
Aug. 1	292	206	1,283	30	4	1,811	0	-50	0	0	661	103	103	558	-50
2	477	206	1,162	0	5	1,845	0	-50	0	0	661	231	334	327	-33
3	0	0	974	190	6	1,164	636	-50	586	586	1,247	717	1,051	196	-20
4	0	89	971	8	7	1,068	732	-50	682	642	1,889	752	1,803	86	-9
5	186	100	909	16	8	1,211	589	-50	539	539	2,428	469	2,272	156	-16
6	186	100	837	50	9	1,173	627	-33	594	594	3,022	557	2,829	193	-19
7	186	0	774	31	10	991	809	-20	789	789	3,811	719	3,548	263	-26
8	186	152	724	7	11	1,069	731	-9	722	717	4,528	807	4,355	173	-17
9	328	113	699	3	12	1,143	657	-16	641	641	5,169	607	4,962	207	-21
10	0	113	701	1	13	815	985	-19	966	967	6,136	1,197	6,159	-23	+2
11	0	0	651	0	14	651	1,149	-26	1,123	1,127	7,263	1,207	7,366	-103	+10
12	160	0	616	0	15	776	1,024	-17	1,007	1,004	8,267	884	8,250	17	-2

MONTAGUE DESIGN RATE = 1,750 (ft³/s) DECEMBER 1, 2005, to DECEMBER 18, 2005

MONTAGUE DESIGN RATE = 1,800 (ft³/s) DECEMBER 19, 2005, to MARCH 15, 2006

MONTAGUE DESIGN RATE = 1,750 (ft³/s) MARCH 16, 2006, to JUNE 14, 2006

MONTAGUE DESIGN RATE = 1,800 (ft³/s) JUNE 15, 2006, to AUGUST 31, 2006

The estimated discharge at Montague was greater than the Montague design rate from December 1, 2005 to July 29, 2006.

Col. 1 - Furnished by power company.
Col. 2 - Furnished by power company.
Col. 3 - Computed from index stations.
Col. 4 - Computed increase in runoff based on quantitative precipitation forecasts.
Col. 5 = Col. 1 + Col. 2 + Col. 3 + Col. 4.

Col. 6 = Design rate - Col. 5, when positive; otherwise Col. 6 = 0.
Col. 7 = Col. 14 (4 days earlier).
Col. 8 = Design rate - Col. 5 + Col. 7, when positive; otherwise Col. 8 = 0.
Col. 9 = Col. 7 from Table 9.
Col. 10 = Summation of Col. 9.

Col. 11 = Design rate - (Col. 9 + Col. 10 from Table 9), when positive; otherwise Col. 11 = 0.
Col. 12 = Summation of Col. 11.
Col. 13 = Col. 10 - Col. 12.
Col. 14 = Col. 13 divided by -10, limited to ±50.

Table 8. New York City reservoir release design data.—Continued
(River Master daily operation record)

[ft³/s, cubic feet per second; (ft³/s)-d, cubic feet per second days; Col., Column]

	Advance estimate of discharge of Delaware River at Montague, New Jersey, exclusive of New York City reservoir releases									Computation of balancing adjustment					
Date of advance estimate	Powerplant release forecasts		Uncontrolled runoff		Montague date	Discharge (ft³/s)	Indicated deficiency	Balancing adjustment (ft³/s)	Directed release (ft³/s)	Adjusted directed release		Actual deficiency		Cumulative difference (ft³/s)-d	Balancing adjustment (ft³/s)
	Lake Wallenpaupack (ft³/s)	Rio Reservoir (ft³/s)	Current condition (ft³/s)	Weather adjustment (ft³/s)						Daily (ft³/s)	Cumulative (ft³/s)-d	Daily (ft³/s)	Cumulative (ft³/s)-d		
2006	Col. 1	Col. 2	Col. 3	Col. 4	2006	Col. 5	Col. 6	Col. 7	Col. 8	Col. 9	Col. 10	Col. 11	Col. 12	Col. 13	Col. 14
Aug. 13	160	0	591	11	Aug. 16	762	1,038	-21	1,017	1,019	9,286	769	9,019	267	-27
14	160	0	571	10	17	741	1,059	+2	1,061	1,061	10,347	851	9,870	477	-48
15	160	0	634	0	18	794	1,006	+10	1,016	1,019	11,366	859	10,729	637	-50
16	160	0	589	0	19	749	1,051	-2	1,049	1,050	12,416	840	11,569	847	-50
17	0	0	529	16	20	545	1,255	-27	1,228	1,228	13,644	1,138	12,707	937	-50
18	0	0	524	187	21	711	1,089	-48	1,041	1,044	14,688	0	12,707	1,981	-50
19	80	0	512	147	22	739	1,061	-50	1,011	1,010	15,698	0	12,707	2,991	-50
20	80	0	1,116	3	23	1,199	601	-50	551	551	16,249	386	13,093	3,156	-50
21	80	60	841	0	24	981	819	-50	769	769	17,018	709	13,802	3,216	-50
22	80	89	727	1	25	897	903	-50	853	851	17,869	851	14,653	3,216	-50
23	80	0	661	16	26	757	1,043	-50	993	992	18,861	712	15,365	3,496	-50
24	0	0	612	20	27	632	1,168	-50	1,118	1,125	19,986	555	15,920	4,066	-50
25	0	0	630	155	28	785	1,015	-50	965	959	20,945	0	15,920	5,025	-50
26	0	0	781	178	29	959	841	-50	791	783	21,728	0	15,920	5,808	-50
27	0	0	855	676	30	1,531	269	-50	219	219	21,947	0	15,920	6,027	-50
28	240	0	1,825	871	31	2,936	0	-50	0	0	21,947	0	15,920	6,027	-50

MONTAGUE DESIGN RATE = 1,750 (ft³/s) SEPTEMBER 1, 2006 to NOVEMBER 30, 2006.

The estimated discharge at Montague was greater than the Montague design rate from September 1, 2006 to November 30, 2006.

Col. 1 - Furnished by power company.
Col. 2 - Furnished by power company.
Col. 3 - Computed from index stations.
Col. 4 - Computed increase in runoff based on quantitative precipitation forecasts.
Col. 5 = Col. 1 + Col. 2 + Col. 3 + Col. 4.

Col. 6 = Design rate - Col. 5, when positive; otherwise Col. 6 = 0.
Col. 7 = Col. 14 (4 days earlier).
Col. 8 = Design rate - Col. 5 + Col. 7, when positive; otherwise Col. 8 = 0.
Col. 9 = Col. 7 from Table 9.
Col. 10 = Summation of Col. 9.

Col. 11 = Design rate - (Col. 9 + Col. 10 from Table 9), when positive; otherwise Col. 11 = 0.
Col. 12 = Summation of Col. 11.
Col. 13 = Col. 10 - Col. 12.
Col. 14 = Col. 13 divided by -10, limited to ±50.

Table 9. Controlled releases from reservoirs in the upper Delaware River Basin and segregation of flow of Delaware River at Montague, New Jersey. (River Master daily operation record)

[Mean discharge in cubic feet per second for 24 hours; Col., Column; Cumul., Cumulative; Do., ditto]

Controlled Releases from New York City Reservoirs					Controlled Releases from Power Reservoirs			Segregation of Flow, Delaware River at Montague, New Jersey							
Directed		Pepacton	Cannonsville	Neversink		Lake Wallenpaupack	Rio Reservoir		Controlled Releases			Computed uncontrolled	Total	Excess Release Credits	
Date 2005	Amount				Date 2005			Date 2005	New York City Reservoirs Directed	Other	Power-plants			Daily	Cumul.
	Col. 1	Col. 2	Col. 3	Col. 4		Col. 5	Col. 6		Col. 7	Col. 8	Col. 9	Col. 10	Col. 11	Col. 12	Col. 13
Nov. 28	0	80	45	25	Nov. 30	384	752	Dec. 1	0	150	1,136	20,314	21,600	Suspended	
29	0	42	46	25	Dec. 1	453	777	2	0	113	1,230	13,057	14,400	Do.	
30	0	36	46	25	2	681	773	3	0	107	1,454	10,139	11,700	Do.	
Dec. 1	0	36	46	25	3	658	773	4	0	107	1,431	8,342	9,880	Do.	
2	0	36	46	25	4	650	787	5	0	107	1,437	7,056	8,600	Do.	
3	0	36	46	25	5	806	777	6	0	107	1,583	5,930	7,620	Do.	
4	0	36	48	25	6	666	762	7	0	109	1,428	5,273	6,810	Do.	
5	0	36	46	25	7	662	741	8	0	107	1,403	4,550	6,060	Do.	
6	0	36	46	25	8	785	408	9	0	107	1,193	4,140	5,440	Do.	
7	0	46	56	25	9	430	67	10	0	127	497	3,876	4,500	Do.	
8	0	87	70	25	10	416	67	11	0	182	483	3,725	4,390	Do.	
9	0	93	71	26	11	280	85	12	0	190	365	3,835	4,390	Do.	
10	0	93	73	25	12	539	128	13	0	191	667	3,342	4,200	Do.	
11	0	93	74	25	13	500	128	14	0	192	628	2,900	3,720	Do.	
12	0	107	87	25	14	552	96	15	0	219	648	2,533	3,400	Do.	
13	0	108	85	25	15	492	0	16	0	218	492	3,590	4,300	Do.	
14	0	108	91	25	16	494	99	17	0	224	593	5,383	6,200	Do.	
15	0	144	122	25	17	469	348	18	0	291	817	5,092	6,200	Do.	
16	0	162	124	25	18	455	135	19	0	311	590	3,999	4,900	0	4,629
17	0	162	108	25	19	526	67	20	0	295	593	3,612	4,500	0	4,629
18	0	139	88	45	20	492	142	21	0	272	634	3,694	4,600	0	4,629
19	0	139	88	68	21	482	191	22	0	295	673	3,332	4,300	0	4,629
20	0	152	128	70	22	509	291	23	0	350	800	3,150	4,300	0	4,629
21	0	155	195	77	23	383	191	24	0	427	574	3,269	4,270	0	4,629
22	0	169	206	77	24	367	202	25	0	452	569	3,149	4,170	0	4,629
23	0	164	187	77	25	449	35	26	0	428	484	5,418	6,330	0	4,629
24	0	164	167	70	26	476	181	27	0	401	657	8,302	9,360	0	4,629
25	0	156	135	46	27	470	191	28	0	337	661	7,472	8,470	0	4,629
26	0	155	91	25	28	430	330	29	0	271	760	6,679	7,710	0	4,629
27	0	116	62	25	29	577	762	30	0	203	1,339	11,158	12,700	0	4,629
28	0	94	46	25	30	621	376	31	0	165	997	12,638	13,800	0	4,629
Total	0	3,180	2,769	1,106		16,154	10,662		0	7,055	26,816	188,949	222,820		

Col. 2 - 24 hours beginning 1200 of date shown.
Col. 3 - 24 hours ending 2400 one day later.
Col. 4 - 24 hours beginning 1500 one day later.
Col. 5 - 24 hours beginning 0800 of date shown.
Col. 6 - 24 hours beginning 1600 of date shown.

Col. 7 = Col. 2 + Col. 3 + Col. 4 in response to direction (Col. 1).
Col. 8 = Col. 2 + Col. 3 + Col. 4 - Col. 7.
Col. 9 = Col. 5 + Col. 6.
Col. 10 = Col. 11 - Col. 7 - Col. 8 - Col. 9.
Col. 11 = 24 hours of calendar day shown.

Col. 12 = Col. 11 - Col. 8 - 1,750 ft³/s computed arithmetically, but not greater than Col. 7; except that part of Col. 8 contributing to the excess-release increment of Col. 11.

Col. 13 = Summation of Col. 12.

Table 9. Controlled releases from reservoirs in the upper Delaware River Basin and segregation of flow of Delaware River at Montague, New Jersey.—Continued (River Master daily operation record)

[Mean discharge in cubic feet per second for 24 hours; Col., Column; Cumul., Cumulative]

Controlled Releases from New York City Reservoirs					Controlled Releases from Power Reservoirs			Segregation of Flow, Delaware River at Montague, New Jersey							
Directed		Pepacton	Cannonsville	Neversink	Date	Lake Wallenpaupack	Rio Reservoir	Date	Controlled Releases			Computed uncontrolled	Total	Excess Release Credits	
Date	Amount								New York City Reservoirs		Power-plants			Daily	Cumul.
									Directed	Other					
2005/2006	Col. 1	Col. 2	Col. 3	Col. 4	2005/2006	Col. 5	Col. 6	2006	Col. 7	Col. 8	Col. 9	Col. 10	Col. 11	Col. 12	Col. 13
Dec. 29	0	36	48	25	Dec. 31	614	755	Jan. 1	0	109	1,369	9,822	11,300	0	4,629
30	0	36	48	25	Jan. 1	644	218	2	0	109	862	8,569	9,540	0	4,629
31	0	36	45	25	2	827	780	3	0	106	1,607	8,147	9,860	0	4,629
Jan. 1	0	36	43	25	3	827	773	4	0	104	1,600	8,006	9,710	0	4,629
2	0	36	46	25	4	825	259	5	0	107	1,084	7,279	8,470	0	4,629
3	0	36	46	25	5	827	362	6	0	107	1,189	7,164	8,460	0	4,629
4	0	36	46	25	6	827	745	7	0	107	1,572	6,191	7,870	0	4,629
5	0	36	46	25	7	827	415	8	0	107	1,242	5,491	6,840	0	4,629
6	0	40	46	25	8	827	397	9	0	111	1,224	4,915	6,250	0	4,629
7	0	71	46	25	9	827	401	10	0	142	1,228	4,430	5,800	0	4,629
8	0	76	46	25	10	827	401	11	0	147	1,228	4,445	5,820	0	4,629
9	0	77	46	25	11	827	394	12	0	148	1,221	7,161	8,530	0	4,629
10	0	84	46	25	12	814	401	13	0	155	1,215	10,230	11,600	0	4,629
11	0	77	45	25	13	827	138	14	0	147	965	13,288	14,400	0	4,629
12	0	36	45	25	14	1,200	709	15	0	106	1,909	30,585	32,600	0	4,629
13	0	36	45	25	15	1,667	738	16	0	106	2,405	21,189	23,700	0	4,629
14	0	36	45	25	16	1,667	794	17	0	106	2,461	16,733	19,300	0	4,629
15	0	36	45	25	17	1,667	766	18	0	106	2,433	24,961	27,500	0	4,629
16	0	36	45	25	18	1,667	773	19	0	106	2,440	54,954	57,500	0	4,629
17	0	36	45	25	19	1,648	741	20	0	106	2,389	36,005	38,500	0	4,629
18	0	36	45	25	20	1,662	770	21	0	106	2,432	25,662	28,200	0	4,629
19	0	36	46	25	21	1,667	773	22	0	107	2,440	20,153	22,700	0	4,629
20	0	36	45	25	22	1,667	773	23	0	106	2,440	17,254	19,800	0	4,629
21	0	36	45	25	23	1,667	770	24	0	106	2,437	15,157	17,700	0	4,629
22	0	36	45	25	24	1,667	773	25	0	106	2,440	13,054	15,600	0	4,629
23	0	36	45	164	25	1,671	766	26	0	245	2,437	10,818	13,500	0	4,629
24	0	249	45	251	26	1,671	770	27	0	545	2,441	8,914	11,900	0	4,629
25	0	640	45	271	27	1,671	762	28	0	956	2,433	7,311	10,700	0	4,629
26	0	794	45	265	28	1,674	752	29	0	1,104	2,426	6,670	10,200	0	4,629
27	0	794	45	257	29	1,674	599	30	0	1,096	2,273	6,831	10,200	0	4,629
28	0	801	45	251	30	1,670	287	31	0	1,097	1,957	8,646	11,700	0	4,629
Total	0	4,423	1,409	2,084		39,044	18,755		0	7,916	57,799	430,035	495,750		

Col. 2 - 24 hours beginning 1200 of date shown.
Col. 3 - 24 hours ending 2400 one day later.
Col. 4 - 24 hours beginning 1500 one day later.
Col. 5 - 24 hours beginning 0800 of date shown.
Col. 6 - 24 hours beginning 1600 of date shown.

Col. 7 = Col. 2 + Col. 3 + Col. 4 in response to direction (Col. 1).
Col. 8 = Col. 2 + Col. 3 + Col. 4 - Col. 7.
Col. 9 = Col. 5 + Col. 6.
Col. 10 = Col. 11 - Col. 7 - Col. 8 - Col. 9.
Col. 11 = 24 hours of calendar day shown.

Col. 12 = Col. 11 - Col. 8 - 1,750 ft³/s computed arithmetically, but not greater than Col. 7; except that part of Col. 8 contributing to the excess-release increment of Col. 11.

Col. 13 = Summation of Col. 12.

Table 9. Controlled releases from reservoirs in the upper Delaware River Basin and segregation of flow of Delaware River at Montague, New Jersey.—Continued (River Master daily operation record)

[Mean discharge in cubic feet per second for 24 hours; Col., Column; Cumul., Cumulative]

Controlled Releases from New York City Reservoirs					Controlled Releases from Power Reservoirs			Segregation of Flow, Delaware River at Montague, New Jersey							
Directed		Pepacton	Cannonsville	Neversink		Lake Wallenpaupack	Rio Reservoir		Controlled Releases		Power-plants	Computed uncontrolled	Total	Excess Release Credits	
Date 2006	Amount				Date 2006			Date 2006	New York City Reservoirs					Daily	Cumul.
									Directed	Other					
	Col. 1	Col. 2	Col. 3	Col. 4		Col. 5	Col. 6		Col. 7	Col. 8	Col. 9	Col. 10	Col. 11	Col. 12	Col. 13
Jan. 29	0	794	45	246	Jan. 31	1,657	397	Feb. 1	0	1,085	2,054	11,861	15,000	0	4,629
30	0	794	45	243	Feb. 1	1,649	564	2	0	1,082	2,213	10,605	13,900	0	4,629
31	0	794	45	227	2	1,299	752	3	0	1,066	2,051	10,983	14,100	0	4,629
Feb. 1	0	794	45	201	3	615	755	4	0	1,040	1,370	18,590	21,000	0	4,629
2	0	794	45	181	4	718	752	5	0	1,020	1,470	20,410	22,900	0	4,629
3	0	794	45	39	5	634	759	6	0	878	1,393	20,329	22,600	0	4,629
4	0	557	45	25	6	537	730	7	0	627	1,267	16,706	18,600	0	4,629
5	0	43	45	25	7	893	730	8	0	113	1,623	14,164	15,900	0	4,629
6	0	36	45	25	8	900	727	9	0	106	1,627	11,567	13,300	0	4,629
7	0	36	45	29	9	738	578	10	0	110	1,316	10,174	11,600	0	4,629
8	0	337	45	141	10	691	699	11	0	523	1,390	8,487	10,400	0	4,629
9	0	764	45	190	11	597	440	12	0	999	1,037	7,294	9,330	0	4,629
10	0	794	45	184	12	696	450	13	0	1,023	1,146	6,301	8,470	0	4,629
11	0	794	45	166	13	668	365	14	0	1,005	1,033	5,802	7,840	0	4,629
12	0	794	45	118	14	729	472	15	0	957	1,201	5,232	7,390	0	4,629
13	0	777	45	176	15	692	454	16	0	998	1,146	4,906	7,050	0	4,629
14	0	811	45	175	16	693	358	17	0	1,031	1,051	5,018	7,100	0	4,629
15	0	794	45	158	17	464	433	18	0	997	897	4,966	6,860	0	4,629
16	0	794	45	25	18	412	351	19	0	864	763	4,373	6,000	0	4,629
17	0	732	45	28	19	330	348	20	0	805	678	3,407	4,890	0	4,629
18	0	278	45	40	20	532	71	21	0	363	603	3,884	4,850	0	4,629
19	0	381	45	40	21	468	78	22	0	466	546	3,598	4,610	0	4,629
20	0	381	45	40	22	466	60	23	0	466	526	3,568	4,560	0	4,629
21	0	381	45	40	23	363	113	24	0	466	476	3,688	4,630	0	4,629
22	0	778	45	40	24	435	113	25	0	863	548	3,019	4,430	0	4,629
23	0	800	45	40	25	0	0	26	0	885	0	2,775	3,660	0	4,629
24	0	800	45	40	26	31	28	27	0	885	59	2,716	3,660	0	4,629
25	0	798	45	40	27	442	85	28	0	883	527	2,390	3,800	0	4,629
Total	0	17,424	1,260	2,922		18,349	11,662		0	21,606	30,011	226,813	278,430		

Col. 2 - 24 hours beginning 1200 of date shown.
Col. 3 - 24 hours ending 2400 one day later.
Col. 4 - 24 hours beginning 1500 one day later.
Col. 5 - 24 hours beginning 0800 of date shown.
Col. 6 - 24 hours beginning 1600 of date shown.

Col. 7 = Col. 2 + Col. 3 + Col. 4 in response to direction (Col. 1).
Col. 8 = Col. 2 + Col. 3 + Col. 4 - Col. 7.
Col. 9 = Col. 5 + Col. 6.
Col. 10 = Col. 11 - Col. 7 - Col. 8 - Col. 9.
Col. 11 = 24 hours of calendar day shown.

Col. 12 = Col. 11 - 1,750 ft³/s computed arithmetically, but not greater than Col. 7; except that part of Col. 8 contributing to the excess-release increment of Col. 11.

Col. 13 = Summation of Col. 12.

Table 9. Controlled releases from reservoirs in the upper Delaware River Basin and segregation of flow of Delaware River at Montague, New Jersey.—Continued

(River Master daily operation record)

[Mean discharge in cubic feet per second for 24 hours; Col., Column; Cumul., Cumulative]

Controlled Releases from New York City Reservoirs					Controlled Releases from Power Reservoirs			Segregation of Flow, Delaware River at Montague, New Jersey							
Directed		Pepacton	Cannonsville	Neversink	Date	Lake Wallenpaupack	Rio Reservoir	Date	Controlled Releases		Power-plants	Computed uncontrolled	Total	Excess Release Credits	
Date 2006	Amount				2006			2006	New York City Reservoirs					Daily	Cumul.
									Directed	Other					
	Col. 1	Col. 2	Col. 3	Col. 4		Col. 5	Col. 6		Col. 7	Col. 8	Col. 9	Col. 10	Col. 11	Col. 12	Col. 13
Feb. 26	0	798	45	73	Feb. 28	442	113	Mar. 1	0	916	555	2,439	3,910	0	4,629
27	0	761	45	93	Mar. 1	410	57	2	0	899	467	2,144	3,510	0	4,629
28	0	248	45	108	2	471	110	3	0	401	581	2,398	3,380	0	4,629
Mar. 1	0	186	45	108	3	465	117	4	0	339	582	2,469	3,390	0	4,629
2	0	186	45	107	4	0	0	5	0	338	0	2,182	2,520	0	4,629
3	0	186	45	107	5	54	46	6	0	338	100	2,432	2,870	0	4,629
4	0	186	45	107	6	565	181	7	0	338	746	2,156	3,240	0	4,629
5	0	186	45	110	7	552	0	8	0	341	552	2,147	3,040	0	4,629
6	0	186	45	110	8	429	0	9	0	341	429	2,160	2,930	0	4,629
7	0	186	57	108	9	456	0	10	0	351	456	2,203	3,010	0	4,629
8	0	186	155	108	10	428	57	11	0	449	485	2,356	3,290	0	4,629
9	0	186	249	94	11	0	0	12	0	529	0	2,391	2,920	0	4,629
10	0	173	255	93	12	11	14	13	0	521	25	2,494	3,040	0	4,629
11	0	170	255	87	13	152	227	14	0	512	379	3,479	4,370	0	4,629
12	0	169	232	59	14	143	227	15	0	460	370	4,540	5,370	0	4,629
13	0	136	164	29	15	132	181	16	0	329	313	4,188	4,830		
14	0	54	48	26	16	157	103	17	0	128	260	4,112	4,500		
15	0	36	48	26	17	176	149	18	0	110	325	3,935	4,370		
16	0	36	48	26	18	0	103	19	0	110	103	3,647	3,860		
17	0	36	48	25	19	0	14	20	0	109	14	3,567	3,690		
18	0	36	48	31	20	171	238	21	0	115	409	3,266	3,790		
19	0	40	48	32	21	157	170	22	0	120	327	3,013	3,460		
20	0	45	46	39	22	128	170	23	0	130	298	2,822	3,250		
21	0	45	46	34	23	156	152	24	0	125	308	2,597	3,030		
22	0	45	46	40	24	99	0	25	0	131	99	2,570	2,800		
23	0	57	46	42	25	0	0	26	0	145	0	2,645	2,790		
24	0	59	46	40	26	0	14	27	0	145	14	2,671	2,830		
25	0	59	46	29	27	119	106	28	0	134	225	2,521	2,880		
26	0	53	46	34	28	133	170	29	0	133	303	2,334	2,770		
27	0	65	45	40	29	201	227	30	0	150	428	2,132	2,710		
28	0	73	45	40	30	132	113	31	0	158	245	2,067	2,470		
Total	0	4,868	2,472	2,005		6,339	3,059		0	9,345	9,398	86,077	104,820		

Col. 2 - 24 hours beginning 1200 of date shown.
Col. 3 - 24 hours ending 2400 one day later.
Col. 4 - 24 hours beginning 1500 one day later.
Col. 5 - 24 hours beginning 0800 of date shown.
Col. 6 - 24 hours beginning 1600 of date shown.

Col. 7 = Col. 2 + Col. 3 + Col. 4 in response to direction (Col. 1).
Col. 8 = Col. 2 + Col. 3 + Col. 4 - Col. 7.
Col. 9 = Col. 5 + Col. 6.
Col. 10 = Col. 11 - Col. 7 - Col. 8 - Col. 9.
Col. 11 = 24 hours of calendar day shown.

Col. 12 = Col. 11 - Col. 8 - 1,750 ft³/s computed arithmetically, but not greater than Col. 7; except that part of Col. 8 contributing to the excess-release increment of Col. 11.

Col. 13 = Summation of Col. 12.

Table 9. Controlled releases from reservoirs in the upper Delaware River Basin and segregation of flow of Delaware River at Montague, New Jersey.—Continued

(River Master daily operation record)

[Mean discharge in cubic feet per second for 24 hours; Col., Column; Cumul., Cumulative]

Controlled Releases from New York City Reservoirs					Controlled Releases from Power Reservoirs			Segregation of Flow, Delaware River at Montague, New Jersey					
Directed		Pepacton	Cannonsville	Neversink		Lake Wallenpaupack	Rio Reservoir		Controlled Releases			Computed uncontrolled	Total
Date 2006	Amount				Date 2006			Date	New York City Reservoirs Directed	New York City Reservoirs Other	Power-plants		
	Col. 1	Col. 2	Col. 3	Col. 4	2006	Col. 5	Col. 6	2006	Col. 7	Col. 8	Col. 9	Col. 10	Col. 11
Mar. 29	0	74	45	42	Mar. 31	152	128	Apr. 1	0	161	280	1,949	2,390
30	0	74	45	48	Apr. 1	0	0	2	0	167	0	2,053	2,220
31	0	74	45	32	2	0	43	3	0	151	43	2,156	2,350
Apr. 1	0	63	42	26	3	0	170	4	0	131	170	2,439	2,740
2	0	57	43	25	4	0	184	5	0	125	184	2,871	3,180
3	0	37	45	20	5	0	167	6	0	102	167	2,951	3,220
4	0	36	45	19	6	1	170	7	0	100	171	2,769	3,040
5	0	26	45	15	7	0	124	8	0	86	124	2,820	3,030
6	0	14	45	15	8	0	0	9	0	74	0	3,216	3,290
7	0	12	45	15	9	0	0	10	0	72	0	3,128	3,200
8	0	12	45	19	10	0	0	11	0	76	0	2,924	3,000
9	0	12	45	23	11	0	18	12	0	80	18	2,822	2,920
10	0	12	45	23	12	5	99	13	0	80	104	2,696	2,880
11	0	12	45	26	13	0	103	14	0	83	103	2,644	2,830
12	0	12	45	32	14	0	128	15	0	89	128	2,813	3,030
13	0	12	45	22	15	0	241	16	0	79	241	3,200	3,520
14	0	12	45	19	16	0	160	17	0	76	160	2,984	3,220
15	0	12	45	25	17	0	170	18	0	82	170	2,718	2,970
16	0	12	45	31	18	0	128	19	0	88	128	2,484	2,700
17	0	12	45	39	19	0	18	20	0	96	18	2,386	2,500
18	0	36	45	39	20	0	89	21	0	120	89	2,151	2,360
19	0	36	45	40	21	0	71	22	0	121	71	2,108	2,300
20	0	28	45	46	22	0	227	23	0	119	227	6,304	6,650
21	0	32	45	19	23	0	415	24	0	96	415	16,589	17,100
22	0	14	45	17	24	0	674	25	0	76	674	17,050	17,800
23	0	12	45	25	25	0	677	26	0	82	677	13,841	14,600
24	0	32	45	25	26	0	631	27	0	102	631	11,767	12,500
25	0	36	45	25	27	0	191	28	0	106	191	9,903	10,200
26	0	36	45	25	28	0	128	29	0	106	128	8,436	8,670
27	0	36	45	25	29	0	0	30	0	106	0	7,384	7,490
Total	0	885	1,345	802		158	5,154		0	3,032	5,312	149,556	157,900

Col. 2 - 24 hours beginning 1200 of date shown.
Col. 3 - 24 hours ending 2400 one day later.
Col. 4 - 24 hours beginning 1500 one day later.
Col. 5 - 24 hours beginning 0800 of date shown.
Col. 6 - 24 hours beginning 1600 of date shown.

Col. 7 = Col. 2 + Col. 3 + Col. 4 in response to direction (Col. 1).
Col. 8 = Col. 2 + Col. 3 + Col. 4 - Col. 7.
Col. 9 = Col. 5 + Col. 6.
Col. 10 = Col. 11 - Col. 7 - Col. 8 - Col. 9.
Col. 11 = 24 hours of calendar day shown.

Table 9. Controlled releases from reservoirs in the upper Delaware River Basin and segregation of flow of Delaware River at Montague, New Jersey.—Continued

(River Master daily operation record)

[Mean discharge in cubic feet per second for 24 hours; Col., Column; Cumul., Cumulative]

Controlled Releases from New York City Reservoirs					Controlled Releases from Power Reservoirs			Segregation of Flow, Delaware River at Montague, New Jersey					
Directed		Pepacton	Cannons-ville	Never-sink		Lake Wallenpaupack	Rio Reservoir		Controlled Releases			Computed uncon-trolled	Total
Date 2006	Amount				Date 2006			Date 2006	New York City Reservoirs		Power-plants		
									Directed	Other			
	Col. 1	Col. 2	Col. 3	Col. 4		Col. 5	Col. 6		Col. 7	Col. 8	Col. 9	Col. 10	Col. 11
Apr. 28	0	36	45	25	Apr. 30	0	131	May 1	0	106	131	6,283	6,520
29	0	36	45	25	May 1	0	202	2	0	106	202	5,382	5,690
30	0	36	45	25	2	0	184	3	0	106	184	4,830	5,120
May 1	0	36	45	25	3	0	202	4	0	106	202	4,342	4,650
2	0	36	45	26	4	15	227	5	0	107	242	3,811	4,160
3	0	36	45	34	5	0	71	6	0	115	71	3,314	3,500
4	0	37	45	45	6	0	0	7	0	127	0	2,973	3,100
5	0	60	45	50	7	0	43	8	0	155	43	2,702	2,900
6	0	71	45	59	8	463	174	9	0	175	637	2,388	3,200
7	0	84	45	63	9	553	145	10	0	192	698	2,200	3,090
8	0	96	45	63	10	1,047	216	11	0	204	1,263	2,093	3,560
9	0	102	45	65	11	1,114	433	12	0	212	1,547	4,001	5,760
10	0	105	45	50	12	249	351	13	0	200	600	5,860	6,660
11	0	85	45	25	13	0	291	14	0	155	291	6,274	6,720
12	0	70	45	25	14	0	0	15	0	140	0	6,070	6,210
13	0	76	45	25	15	941	135	16	0	146	1,076	5,948	7,170
14	0	36	45	25	16	652	241	17	0	106	893	8,191	9,190
15	0	36	45	25	17	762	227	18	0	106	989	7,755	8,850
16	0	36	45	25	18	752	284	19	0	106	1,036	6,988	8,130
17	0	36	45	25	19	276	174	20	0	106	450	7,734	8,290
18	0	36	45	25	20	0	230	21	0	106	230	7,014	7,350
19	0	36	45	25	21	0	284	22	0	106	284	6,250	6,640
20	0	36	45	25	22	143	525	23	0	106	668	5,576	6,350
21	0	37	45	25	23	171	227	24	0	107	398	5,285	5,790
22	0	36	45	25	24	212	227	25	0	106	439	4,765	5,310
23	0	37	45	31	25	201	145	26	0	113	346	4,621	5,080
24	0	36	45	111	26	208	46	27	0	192	254	5,024	5,470
25	0	36	45	25	27	0	71	28	0	106	71	4,943	5,120
26	0	36	45	25	28	0	241	29	0	106	241	4,153	4,500
27	0	36	45	36	29	0	230	30	0	117	230	3,513	3,860
28	0	45	51	73	30	0	213	31	0	169	213	4,498	4,880
Total	0	1,553	1,401	1,156	Total	7,759	6,170	Total	0	4,110	13,929	154,781	172,820

Col. 2 - 24 hours beginning 1200 of date shown.
Col. 3 - 24 hours ending 2400 one day later.
Col. 4 - 24 hours beginning 1500 one day later.
Col. 5 - 24 hours beginning 0800 of date shown.
Col. 6 - 24 hours beginning 1600 of date shown.

Col. 7 = Col. 2 + Col. 3 + Col. 4 in response to direction (Col. 1).
Col. 8 = Col. 2 + Col. 3 + Col. 4 - Col. 7.
Col. 9 = Col. 5 + Col. 6.
Col. 10 = Col. 11 - Col. 7 - Col. 8 - Col. 9.
Col. 11 = 24 hours of calendar day shown.

Table 9. Controlled releases from reservoirs in the upper Delaware River Basin and segregation of flow of Delaware River at Montague, New Jersey.—Continued (River Master daily operation record)

[Mean discharge in cubic feet per second for 24 hours; Col., Column; Cumul., Cumulative]

Controlled Releases from New York City Reservoirs					Controlled Releases from Power Reservoirs			Segregation of Flow, Delaware River at Montague, New Jersey							
Directed		Pepacton	Cannonsville	Neversink		Lake Wallenpaupack	Rio Reservoir		Controlled Releases			Computed uncontrolled	Total	Excess Release Credits	
Date 2006	Amount				Date 2006			Date 2006	New York City Reservoirs		Power-plants			Daily	Cumul.
									Directed	Other					
	Col. 1	Col. 2	Col. 3	Col. 4		Col. 5	Col. 6		Col. 7	Col. 8	Col. 9	Col. 10	Col. 11	Col. 12	Col. 13
May 29	0	234	153	71	May 31	561	674	June 1	0	458	1,235	5,457	7,150		
30	0	391	130	25	June 1	878	674	2	0	546	1,552	4,432	6,530		
31	0	39	353	25	2	379	149	3	0	417	528	4,335	5,280		
June 1	0	36	308	25	3	0	0	4	0	369	0	7,051	7,420		
2	0	36	308	25	4	0	35	5	0	369	35	7,436	7,840		
3	0	36	308	25	5	478	273	6	0	369	751	6,170	7,290		
4	0	36	308	25	6	447	184	7	0	369	631	5,370	6,370		
5	0	36	308	25	7	968	365	8	0	369	1,333	6,668	8,370		
6	0	36	308	25	8	971	596	9	0	369	1,567	6,704	8,640		
7	0	36	235	25	9	198	291	10	0	296	489	6,675	7,460		
8	0	36	156	25	10	0	170	11	0	217	170	6,853	7,240		
9	0	36	155	25	11	11	177	12	0	216	188	6,776	7,180		
10	0	36	155	25	12	518	103	13	0	216	621	6,263	7,100		
11	0	36	201	46	13	579	156	14	0	283	735	5,622	6,640		
12	0	131	309	46	14	505	152	15	0	486	657	5,137	6,280	0	0
13	0	155	309	46	15	562	152	16	0	510	714	5,176	6,400	0	0
14	0	155	357	50	16	296	64	17	0	562	360	4,618	5,540	0	0
15	0	220	535	71	17	0	0	18	0	826	0	3,944	4,770	0	0
16	0	384	692	116	18	1	89	19	0	1,192	90	3,088	4,370	0	0
17	0	387	775	105	19	325	124	20	0	1,267	449	2,414	4,130	0	0
18	0	238	651	77	20	380	149	21	0	966	529	2,395	3,890	0	0
19	0	156	419	71	21	519	149	22	0	646	668	2,236	3,550	0	0
20	0	93	303	57	22	537	238	23	0	453	775	2,112	3,340	0	0
21	0	77	305	77	23	529	106	24	0	459	635	1,946	3,040	0	0
22	0	77	268	77	24	0	0	25	0	422	0	2,508	2,930	0	0
23	0	77	450	77	25	92	206	26	0	604	298	11,398	12,300	0	0
24	0	77	467	74	26	1,460	603	27	0	618	2,063	55,719	58,400	0	0
25	0	77	402	32	27	1,681	631	28	0	511	2,312	159,177	162,000	0	0
26	0	42	192	25	28	1,667	649	29	0	259	2,316	153,425	156,000	0	0
27	0	42	71	25	29	1,693	649	30	0	138	2,342	65,620	68,100	0	0
Total	0	3,448	9,891	1,443		16,235	7,808		0	14,782	24,043	566,725	605,550		

Col. 2 - 24 hours beginning 1200 of date shown.
Col. 3 - 24 hours ending 2400 one day later.
Col. 4 - 24 hours beginning 1500 one day later.
Col. 5 - 24 hours beginning 0800 of date shown.
Col. 6 - 24 hours beginning 1600 of date shown.

Col. 7 = Col. 2 + Col. 3 + Col. 4 in response to direction (Col. 1).
Col. 8 = Col. 2 + Col. 3 + Col. 4 - Col. 7.
Col. 9 = Col. 5 + Col. 6.
Col. 10 = Col. 11 - Col. 7 - Col. 8 - Col. 9.
Col. 11 = 24 hours of calendar day shown.

Col. 12 = Col. 11 - Col. 8 - 1,750 ft³/s computed arithmetically, but not greater than Col. 7; except that part of Col. 8 contributing to the excess-release increment of Col. 11.

Col. 13 = Season limit of cumulative credit beginning June 15, 2006 = 11,418 (ft³/s)-d. A total of 5,718 (ft³/s)-d is available for release.

Table 9. Controlled releases from reservoirs in the upper Delaware River Basin and segregation of flow of Delaware River at Montague, New Jersey.—Continued

(River Master daily operation record)

[Mean discharge in cubic feet per second for 24 hours: Col., Column; Cumul., Cumulative]

Controlled Releases from New York City Reservoirs					Controlled Releases from Power Reservoirs				Segregation of Flow, Delaware River at Montague, New Jersey						
Directed		New York City Reservoirs				Lake Wallenpaupack	Rio Reservoir		Controlled Releases			Computed uncontrolled	Total	Excess Release Credits	
Date 2006	Amount	Pepacton	Cannonsville	Neversink	Date 2006			Date 2006	New York City Reservoirs		Power-plants			Daily	Cumul.
									Directed	Other					
	Col. 1	Col. 2	Col. 3	Col. 4		Col. 5	Col. 6		Col. 7	Col. 8	Col. 9	Col. 10	Col. 11	Col. 12	Col. 13
June 28	0	36	60	25	June 30	1,703	645	July 1	0	121	2,348	37,031	39,500	0	0
29	0	36	60	25	July 1	1,721	645	2	0	121	2,366	24,713	27,200	0	0
30	0	36	60	65	2	1,721	645	3	0	161	2,366	17,573	20,100	0	0
July 1	0	36	60	76	3	1,721	642	4	0	172	2,363	13,665	16,200	0	0
2	0	42	367	90	4	1,721	638	5	0	499	2,359	10,542	13,400	0	0
3	0	107	736	67	5	1,724	635	6	0	910	2,359	7,831	11,100	0	0
4	0	107	735	25	6	1,724	624	7	0	867	2,348	6,185	9,400	0	0
5	0	107	585	25	7	1,695	613	8	0	717	2,308	5,285	8,310	0	0
6	0	108	466	54	8	1,726	631	9	0	628	2,357	4,595	7,580	0	0
7	0	131	551	77	9	1,731	628	10	0	759	2,359	3,812	6,930	0	0
8	0	153	673	87	10	1,334	571	11	0	913	1,905	2,982	5,800	0	0
9	0	155	537	67	11	678	631	12	0	759	1,309	2,762	4,830	0	0
10	0	63	351	60	12	563	628	13	0	474	1,191	2,975	4,640	0	0
11	0	45	354	77	13	431	493	14	0	476	924	3,360	4,760	0	0
12	0	114	371	77	14	576	135	15	0	562	711	2,857	4,130	0	0
13	0	77	455	104	15	453	0	16	0	636	453	2,841	3,930	0	0
14	0	97	665	124	16	447	67	17	0	886	514	2,460	3,860	0	0
15	0	124	696	124	17	387	138	18	0	944	525	2,071	3,540	0	0
16	0	124	696	124	18	400	156	19	0	944	556	1,800	3,300	0	0
17	0	124	696	119	19	433	167	20	0	939	600	1,601	3,140	0	0
18	0	124	602	101	20	496	152	21	0	827	648	1,605	3,080	0	0
19	0	153	419	101	21	561	89	22	0	673	650	1,937	3,260	0	0
20	0	170	387	101	22	159	0	23	0	658	159	2,773	3,590	0	0
21	0	170	317	42	23	15	0	24	0	529	15	2,696	3,240	0	0
22	0	105	159	67	24	511	92	25	0	331	603	2,246	3,180	0	0
23	0	162	204	77	25	643	160	26	0	443	803	1,844	3,090	0	0
24	0	170	252	104	26	517	152	27	0	526	669	1,685	2,880	0	0
25	0	178	309	108	27	453	181	28	0	595	634	1,681	2,910	0	0
26	0	193	309	105	28	568	35	29	0	607	603	1,670	2,880	0	0
27	281	192	309	93	29	150	0	30	281	313	150	1,796	2,540	281	281
28	380	162	309	93	30	270	60	31	380	184	330	1,836	2,730	380	661
Total	661	3,601	12,750	2,484		27,232	10,253		661	18,174	37,485	178,710	235,030		

Col. 2 - 24 hours beginning 1200 of date shown.
Col. 3 - 24 hours ending 2400 one day later.
Col. 4 - 24 hours beginning 1500 one day later.
Col. 5 - 24 hours beginning 0800 of date shown.
Col. 6 - 24 hours beginning 1600 of date shown.

Col. 7 = Col. 2 + Col. 3 + Col. 4 in response to direction (Col. 1).
Col. 8 = Col. 2 + Col. 3 + Col. 4 - Col. 7.
Col. 9 = Col. 5 + Col. 6.
Col. 10 = Col. 11 - Col. 7 - Col. 8 - Col. 9.
Col. 11 = 24 hours of calendar day shown.

Col. 12 = Col. 11 - Col. 8 - 1,750 ft³/s computed arithmetically, but not greater than Col. 7; except that part of Col. 8 contributing to the excess-release increment of Col. 11.

Col. 13 = Season limit of cumulative credit beginning June 15, 2006 = 11,418 (ft³/s)-d. A total of 5,718 (ft³/s)-d is available for release.

Table 9. Controlled releases from reservoirs in the upper Delaware River Basin and segregation of flow of Delaware River at Montague, New Jersey.—Continued

(River Master daily operation record)

[Mean discharge in cubic feet per second for 24 hours; Col., Column; Cumul., Cumulative]

Controlled Releases from New York City Reservoirs

Directed Date 2006	Directed Amount Col. 1	Pepacton Col. 2	Cannonsville Col. 3	Neversink Col. 4
July 29	0	128	309	94
30	0	101	435	172
31	0	156	572	201
Aug. 1	0	183	662	128
2	0	150	603	108
3	586	139	480	108
4	682	153	381	108
5	539	156	435	108
6	594	170	459	108
7	789	170	511	108
8	722	170	439	108
9	641	178	385	114
10	966	184	665	118
11	1,123	186	817	124
12	1,007	192	688	124
13	1,017	193	702	124
14	1,061	193	744	124
15	1,016	193	702	124
16	1,049	193	733	124
17	1,228	193	911	124
18	1,041	195	724	125
19	1,011	192	696	122
20	551	125	449	122
21	769	124	521	124
22	853	77	613	161
23	993	80	787	125
24	1,118	108	893	124
25	965	108	729	122
26	791	107	552	124
27	219	105	266	62
28	0	82	153	51
Total	21,331	4,684	18,016	3,713

Controlled Releases from Power Reservoirs

Date 2006	Lake Wallenpaupack Col. 5	Rio Reservoir Col. 6
July 31	722	124
Aug. 1	342	202
2	246	309
3	258	163
4	375	0
5	0	0
6	0	35
7	258	106
8	304	0
9	178	0
10	142	0
11	427	0
12	0	0
13	0	0
14	172	0
15	207	85
16	203	60
17	183	85
18	241	64
19	2	0
20	0	0
21	143	0
22	132	0
23	124	0
24	91	0
25	127	0
26	0	0
27	4	0
28	359	85
29	835	121
30	1,206	149
Total	7,281	1,588

Segregation of Flow, Delaware River at Montague, New Jersey

Date 2006	Controlled Releases NYC Reservoirs Directed Col. 7	Controlled Releases NYC Reservoirs Other Col. 8	Power-plants Col. 9	Computed uncontrolled Col. 10	Total Col. 11	Excess Release Credits Daily Col. 12	Excess Release Credits Cumul. Col. 13
Aug. 1	0	531	846	1,783	3,160	0	661
2	0	708	544	1,678	2,930	0	661
3	0	929	555	1,436	2,920	0	661
4	0	973	421	1,276	2,670	50	711
5	0	861	375	1,194	2,430	50	761
6	586	141	0	1,083	1,810	50	811
7	642		35	1,013	1,690	-60	751
8	539	160	364	967	2,030	120	871
9	594	143	304	939	1,980	87	958
10	789	0	178	903	1,870	120	1,078
11	717	0	142	851	1,710	-40	1,038
12	641	36	427	766	1,870	84	1,122
13	967	0	0	603	1,570	-180	942
14	1,127	0	0	593	1,720	-30	912
15	1,004	0	172	744	1,920	170	1,082
16	1,019	0	292	739	2,050	300	1,382
17	1,061	0	263	686	2,010	260	1,642
18	1,019	0	268	673	1,960	210	1,852
19	1,050	0	305	655	2,010	260	2,112
20	1,228	0	2	660	1,890	140	2,252
21	1,044	0	0	1,876	2,920	1,044	3,296
22	1,010	0	143	1,717	2,870	1,010	4,306
23	551	145	132	1,282	2,110	215	4,521
24	769	0	124	967	1,860	110	4,631
25	851	0	91	858	1,800	50	4,681
26	992	0	127	961	2,080	330	5,011
27	1,125	0	0	1,245	2,370	620	5,631
28	959	0	4	2,047	3,010	87	5,718
29	783	0	444	3,053	4,280	Expired	
30	219	214	956	8,811	10,200		
31	0	286	1,355	8,229	9,870		
Total	21,286	5,127	8,869	50,288	85,570		

Col. 2 - 24 hours beginning 1200 of date shown.
Col. 3 - 24 hours ending 2400 one day later.
Col. 4 - 24 hours beginning 1500 one day later.
Col. 5 - 24 hours beginning 0800 of date shown.
Col. 6 - 24 hours beginning 1600 of date shown.

Col. 7 = Col. 2 + Col. 3 + Col. 4 in response to direction (Col. 1).
Col. 8 = Col. 2 + Col. 3 + Col. 4 - Col. 7.
Col. 9 = Col. 5 + Col. 6.
Col. 10 = Col. 11 - Col. 7 - Col. 8 - Col. 9.
Col. 11 = 24 hours of calendar day shown.

Col. 12 = Col. 11 - Col. 8 - 1,750 ft³/s computed arithmetically, but not greater than Col. 7; except that part of Col. 8 contributing to the excess-release increment of Col. 11.

Col. 13 = Season limit of cumulative credit beginning June 15, 2006 = 11,418 (ft³/s)-d. A total of 5,718 (ft³/s)-d is available for release.

Table 9. Controlled releases from reservoirs in the upper Delaware River Basin and segregation of flow of Delaware River at Montague, New Jersey.—Continued

(River Master daily operation record)

[Mean discharge in cubic feet per second for 24 hours; Col., Column; Cumul., Cumulative]

Controlled Releases from New York City Reservoirs					Controlled Releases from Power Reservoirs			Segregation of Flow, Delaware River at Montague, New Jersey							
Directed		Pepacton	Cannonsville	Neversink	Date	Lake Wallenpaupack	Rio Reservoir	Date	Controlled Releases			Computed uncontrolled	Total	Excess Release Credits	
Date	Amount								New York City Reservoirs		Power-plants			Daily	Cumul.
2006	Col. 1	Col. 2	Col. 3	Col. 4	2006	Col. 5	Col. 6	2006	Directed Col. 7	Other Col. 8	Col. 9	Col. 10	Col. 11	Col. 12	Col. 13
Aug. 29	0	37	99	25	Aug. 31	1,480	248	Sept. 1	0	161	1,728	5,081	6,970		
30	0	36	156	25	Sept. 1	1,579	110	2	0	217	1,689	4,304	6,210		
31	0	36	161	25	2	797	32	3	0	222	829	4,839	5,890		
Sept. 1	0	36	161	25	3	471	0	4	0	222	471	4,377	5,070		
2	0	36	155	25	4	2	0	5	0	216	2	3,992	4,210		
3	0	36	159	25	5	507	89	6	0	220	596	3,554	4,370		
4	0	36	158	25	6	482	152	7	0	219	634	3,167	4,020		
5	0	36	156	25	7	781	152	8	0	217	933	2,730	3,880		
6	0	50	153	28	8	785	149	9	0	231	934	2,405	3,570		
7	0	76	156	50	9	757	152	10	0	282	909	2,179	3,370		
8	0	93	156	70	10	620	145	11	0	319	765	2,016	3,100		
9	0	108	156	71	11	705	149	12	0	335	854	1,811	3,000		
10	0	119	156	85	12	721	149	13	0	360	870	1,640	2,870		
11	0	136	155	85	13	738	64	14	0	376	802	1,612	2,790		
12	0	139	155	85	14	738	89	15	0	379	827	6,614	7,820		
13	0	139	155	48	15	786	596	16	0	342	1,382	12,876	14,600		
14	0	108	155	25	16	787	241	17	0	288	1,028	8,984	10,300		
15	0	80	155	25	17	776	53	18	0	260	829	6,781	7,870		
16	0	56	155	25	18	816	220	19	0	236	1,036	5,428	6,700		
17	0	56	155	25	19	866	206	20	0	236	1,072	4,772	6,080		
18	0	70	153	25	20	913	280	21	0	248	1,193	4,169	5,610		
19	0	71	156	25	21	909	245	22	0	252	1,154	3,624	5,030		
20	0	87	155	40	22	913	206	23	0	282	1,119	3,189	4,590		
21	0	108	398	51	23	913	149	24	0	557	1,062	3,201	4,820		
22	0	124	998	51	24	913	142	25	0	1,173	1,055	2,592	4,820		
23	0	124	998	57	25	913	206	26	0	1,179	1,119	2,232	4,530		
24	0	124	998	74	26	914	188	27	0	1,196	1,102	1,932	4,230		
25	0	99	998	74	27	914	199	28	0	1,171	1,113	1,806	4,090		
26	0	101	998	74	28	914	199	29	0	1,173	1,113	4,504	6,790		
27	0	101	995	74	29	914	184	30	0	1,170	1,098	8,032	10,300		
Total	0	2,458	9,914	1,367		24,324	4,994		0	13,739	29,318	124,443	167,500		

Col. 2 - 24 hours beginning 1200 of date shown.
Col. 3 - 24 hours ending 2400 one day later.
Col. 4 - 24 hours beginning 1500 one day later.
Col. 5 - 24 hours beginning 0800 of date shown.
Col. 6 - 24 hours beginning 1600 of date shown.

Col. 7 = Col. 2 + Col. 3 + Col. 4 in response to direction (Col. 1).
Col. 8 = Col. 2 + Col. 3 + Col. 4 - Col. 7.
Col. 9 = Col. 5 + Col. 6.
Col. 10 = Col. 11 - Col. 7 - Col. 8 - Col. 9.
Col. 11 = 24 hours of calendar day shown.

Col. 12 = Col. 11 - Col. 8 - 1,750 ft³/s computed arithmetically, but not greater than Col. 7; except that part of Col. 8 contributing to the excess-release increment of Col. 11.

Col. 13 = Season limit of cumulative credit beginning June 15, 2006 = 11,418 (ft³/s)-d. A total of 5,718 (ft³/s)-d is available for release.

Table 9. Controlled releases from reservoirs in the upper Delaware River Basin and segregation of flow of Delaware River at Montague, New Jersey.—Continued
(River Master daily operation record)

[Mean discharge in cubic feet per second for 24 hours; Col., Column; Cumul., Cumulative]

Controlled Releases from New York City Reservoirs					Controlled Releases from Power Reservoirs			Segregation of Flow, Delaware River at Montague, New Jersey							
Directed		Pepacton	Cannonsville	Neversink	Date	Lake Wallenpaupack	Rio Reservoir	Date	Controlled Releases		Power-plants	Computed uncontrolled	Total	Excess Release Credits	
Date 2006	Amount				2006			2006	New York City Reservoirs Directed	New York City Reservoirs Other				Daily	Cumul.
	Col. 1	Col. 2	Col. 3	Col. 4		Col. 5	Col. 6		Col. 7	Col. 8	Col. 9	Col. 10	Col. 11	Col. 12	Col. 13
Sept. 28	0	101	1,002	74	Sept. 30	914	195	Oct. 1	0	1,177	1,109	5,654	7,940		
29	0	101	1,004	71	Oct. 1	914	60	2	0	1,176	974	5,480	7,630		
30	0	97	1,006	65	2	848	14	3	0	1,168	862	5,080	7,110		
Oct. 1	0	85	1,004	65	3	916	152	4	0	1,154	1,068	4,128	6,350		
2	0	85	1,004	65	4	916	152	5	0	1,154	1,068	3,698	5,920		
3	0	85	1,002	65	5	916	152	6	0	1,152	1,068	3,380	5,600		
4	0	85	1,002	65	6	761	142	7	0	1,152	903	3,045	5,100		
5	0	85	999	65	7	578	149	8	0	1,149	727	2,744	4,620		
6	0	85	999	65	8	511	64	9	0	1,149	575	2,506	4,230		
7	0	85	999	65	9	287	78	10	0	1,149	365	2,336	3,850		
8	0	85	999	65	10	300	64	11	0	1,149	364	2,187	3,700		
9	0	85	999	77	11	274	0	12	0	1,161	274	2,395	3,850		
10	0	97	998	74	12	275	0	13	0	1,169	275	2,316	3,760		
11	0	99	517	65	13	272	0	14	0	681	272	2,497	3,450		
12	0	101	998	65	14	0	0	15	0	1,164	0	2,096	3,260		
13	0	111	996	65	15	14	0	16	0	1,172	14	1,924	3,110		
14	0	116	998	65	16	11	25	17	0	1,179	36	2,025	3,240		
15	0	125	996	65	17	0	206	18	0	1,186	206	3,888	5,280		
16	0	131	996	65	18	0	202	19	0	1,192	202	5,376	6,770		
17	0	116	996	65	19	30	206	20	0	1,177	236	4,727	6,140		
18	0	88	1,001	65	20	0	199	21	0	1,154	199	12,647	14,000		
19	0	105	1,006	65	21	0	202	22	0	1,176	202	10,422	11,800		
20	0	97	1,006	65	22	0	309	23	0	1,168	309	7,613	9,090		
21	0	186	1,002	65	23	0	262	24	0	1,253	262	6,045	7,560		
22	0	186	999	65	24	0	220	25	0	1,250	220	5,080	6,550		
23	0	186	999	65	25	0	262	26	0	1,250	262	4,408	5,920		
24	0	186	999	65	26	0	245	27	0	1,250	245	3,955	5,450		
25	0	186	999	65	27	0	436	28	0	1,250	436	8,314	10,000		
26	0	186	1,001	84	28	0	599	29	0	1,271	599	27,730	29,600		
27	0	186	1,001	26	29	0	613	30	0	1,213	613	17,474	19,300		
28	0	266	1,001	159	30	0	624	31	0	1,426	624	12,950	15,000		
Total	0	3,818	30,528	2,125		8,737	5,832		0	36,471	14,569	184,120	235,160		

Col. 2 - 24 hours beginning 1200 of date shown.
Col. 3 - 24 hours ending 2400 one day later.
Col. 4 - 24 hours beginning 1500 one day later.
Col. 5 - 24 hours beginning 0800 of date shown.
Col. 6 - 24 hours beginning 1600 of date shown.

Col. 7 = Col. 2 + Col. 3 + Col. 4 in response to direction (Col. 1).
Col. 8 = Col. 2 + Col. 3 + Col. 4 - Col. 7.
Col. 9 = Col. 5 + Col. 6.
Col. 10 = Col. 11 - Col. 7 - Col. 8 - Col. 9.
Col. 11 = 24 hours of calendar day shown.

Col. 12 = Col. 11 - Col. 8 - 1,750 ft³/s computed arithmetically, but not greater than Col. 7; except that part of Col. 8 contributing to the excess-release increment of Col. 11.
Col. 13 = Season limit of cumulative credit beginning June 15, 2006 = 11,418 (ft³/s)-d. A total of 5,718 (ft³/s)-d is available for release.

Table 9. Controlled releases from reservoirs in the upper Delaware River Basin and segregation of flow of Delaware River at Montague, New Jersey.—Continued (River Master daily operation record)

[Mean discharge in cubic feet per second for 24 hours; Col., Column; Cumul., Cumulative]

Controlled Releases from New York City Reservoirs					Controlled Releases from Power Reservoirs			Segregation of Flow, Delaware River at Montague, New Jersey							
Directed		Pepacton	Cannonsville	Neversink	Date	Lake Wallenpaupack	Rio Reservoir	Date	Controlled Releases			Computed uncontrolled	Total	Excess Release Credits	
Date 2006	Amount				2006			2006	New York City Reservoirs		Power-plants			Daily	Cumul.
									Directed	Other					
	Col. 1	Col. 2	Col. 3	Col. 4		Col. 5	Col. 6		Col. 7	Col. 8	Col. 9	Col. 10	Col. 11	Col. 12	Col. 13
Oct. 29	0	698	1,004	190	Oct. 31	0	610	Nov. 1	0	1,892	610	9,898	12,400		
30	0	699	851	192	Nov. 1	0	624	2	0	1,742	624	9,334	11,700		
31	0	699	668	192	2	0	454	3	0	1,559	454	9,887	11,900		
Nov. 1	0	699	498	192	3	0	376	4	0	1,389	376	8,235	10,000		
2	0	699	565	192	4	0	333	5	0	1,456	333	7,131	8,920		
3	0	699	809	192	5	0	316	6	0	1,700	316	6,154	8,170		
4	0	699	962	192	6	0	298	7	0	1,853	298	5,339	7,490		
5	0	699	999	192	7	0	426	8	0	1,890	426	5,694	8,010		
6	0	699	1,001	193	8	0	649	9	0	1,893	649	13,358	15,900		
7	0	699	999	57	9	0	741	10	0	1,755	741	11,304	13,800		
8	0	699	1,001	97	10	2	741	11	0	1,797	743	8,860	11,400		
9	0	699	1,001	190	11	4	741	12	0	1,890	745	7,565	10,200		
10	0	699	1,001	190	12	14	730	13	0	1,890	744	6,856	9,490		
11	0	699	1,001	190	13	0	720	14	0	1,890	720	6,650	9,260		
12	0	699	999	190	14	0	709	15	0	1,888	709	6,563	9,160		
13	0	699	999	190	15	30	344	16	0	1,888	374	6,198	8,460		
14	0	699	999	190	16	56	681	17	0	1,888	737	26,575	29,200		
15	0	699	993	70	17	757	355	18	0	1,762	1,112	26,026	28,900		
16	0	693	336	25	18	829	727	19	0	1,054	1,556	18,790	21,400		
17	0	429	45	25	19	829	738	20	0	499	1,567	15,434	17,500		
18	0	405	45	25	20	829	695	21	0	475	1,524	12,601	14,600		
19	0	679	45	25	21	829	482	22	0	749	1,311	10,140	12,200		
20	0	699	45	111	22	829	521	23	0	855	1,350	9,695	11,900		
21	0	699	162	158	23	815	535	24	0	1,019	1,350	12,431	14,800		
22	0	699	390	190	24	795	486	25	0	1,279	1,281	10,240	12,800		
23	0	699	582	190	25	829	401	26	0	1,471	1,230	8,599	11,300		
24	0	699	800	190	26	829	401	27	0	1,689	1,230	7,481	10,400		
25	0	699	1,001	190	27	829	443	28	0	1,890	1,272	6,388	9,550		
26	0	699	1,001	190	28	829	507	29	0	1,890	1,336	5,574	8,800		
27	0	684	999	190	29	829	504	30	0	1,873	1,333	4,704	7,910		
Total	0	20,364	21,801	4,600	Total	10,763	16,288	Total	0	46,765	27,051	303,704	377,520		

Col. 2 - 24 hours beginning 1200 of date shown.
Col. 3 - 24 hours ending 2400 one day later.
Col. 4 - 24 hours beginning 1500 one day later.
Col. 5 - 24 hours beginning 0800 of date shown.
Col. 6 - 24 hours beginning 1600 of date shown.

Col. 7 = Col. 2 + Col. 3 + Col. 4 in response to direction (Col. 1).
Col. 8 = Col. 2 + Col. 3 + Col. 4 - Col. 7.
Col. 9 = Col. 5 + Col. 6.
Col. 10 = Col. 11 - Col. 7 - Col. 8 - Col. 9.
Col. 11 = 24 hours of calendar day shown.

Col. 12 = Col. 11 - Col. 8 - 1,750 ft³/s computed arithmetically, but not greater than Col. 7; except that part of Col. 8 contributing to the excess-release increment of Col. 11.

Col. 13 = Season limit of cumulative credit beginning June 15, 2006 = 11,418 (ft³/s)-d. A total of 5,718 (ft³/s)-d is available for release.

Table 10. Diversions to New York City water-supply system. (River Master daily operation record)

[Million gallons per day for 24-hour period beginning 0800 local time]

Date 2005	East Delaware Tunnel	West Delaware Tunnel	Neversink Tunnel	Average June 1, 2005, to date	Date 2006	East Delaware Tunnel	West Delaware Tunnel	Neversink Tunnel	Average June 1, 2005, to date
Dec. 1	0	0	0	599	Jan. 1	0	0	273	554
2	0	0	0	596	2	0	0	272	552
3	0	0	0	593	3	0	0	272	551
4	0	0	0	590	4	0	0	272	550
5	0	0	0	587	5	0	0	272	548
6	0	0	0	584	6	0	0	272	547
7	0	0	0	580	7	0	0	272	546
8	0	0	261	579	8	0	0	272	545
9	0	0	272	577	9	0	0	272	544
10	0	0	273	576	10	0	0	272	542
11	0	0	272	574	11	0	0	43	540
12	0	0	272	573	12	0	0	0	538
13	57	0	272	571	13	0	0	0	535
14	0	0	263	570	14	0	0	0	533
15	0	0	272	568	15	0	0	0	531
16	414	0	148	568	16	0	0	0	528
17	450	0	0	568	17	0	0	0	526
18	452	0	0	567	18	0	0	0	524
19	452	0	0	566	19	0	0	0	522
20	453	0	0	566	20	0	0	0	519
21	453	0	0	565	21	0	0	0	517
22	452	0	0	565	22	0	0	0	515
23	451	0	0	564	23	0	0	0	513
24	451	0	0	564	24	0	0	0	511
25	239	0	0	562	25	0	0	0	508
26	0	0	0	559	26	0	0	0	506
27	388	0	0	559	27	0	0	0	504
28	452	0	0	558	28	0	0	0	502
29	450	0	0	558	29	0	0	0	500
30	0	0	273	556	30	0	0	0	498
31	0	0	273	555	31	0	0	0	496
Total	5,614	0	2,851		Total	0	0	2,764	

Table 10. Diversions to New York City water-supply system.—Continued
(River Master daily operation record)

[Million gallons per day for 24-hour period beginning 0800 local time]

Date 2006	East Delaware Tunnel	West Delaware Tunnel	Neversink Tunnel	Average June 1, 2005, to date
Feb. 1	0	0	0	494
2	0	0	0	492
3	0	0	0	490
4	0	0	0	488
5	0	0	0	486
6	0	0	0	484
7	0	0	0	482
8	0	0	0	480
9	0	0	268	479
10	0	0	6	478
11	0	0	206	477
12	0	0	272	476
13	0	0	2	474
14	0	0	0	472
15	0	0	0	470
16	0	0	193	469
17	0	0	367	469
18	0	0	396	469
19	0	0	396	468
20	0	0	380	468
21	0	0	123	467
22	0	0	0	465
23	0	0	0	463
24	0	0	0	461
25	0	0	0	460
26	0	0	0	458
27	288	0	212	458
28	452	0	406	460
Total	740	0	3,227	

Date 2006	East Delaware Tunnel	West Delaware Tunnel	Neversink Tunnel	Average June 1, 2005, to date
Mar. 1	452	0	98	460
2	493	0	0	460
3	496	0	184	461
4	501	0	274	462
5	501	0	274	463
6	84	0	274	463
7	1	0	274	462
8	1	283	274	462
9	0	301	275	463
10	0	301	329	463
11	0	301	408	464
12	0	301	408	465
13	272	114	407	466
14	452	0	407	468
15	426	0	358	469
16	452	0	415	470
17	346	0	414	471
18	450	0	414	473
19	455	0	414	474
20	433	142	96	475
21	457	157	0	475
22	457	152	0	475
23	458	200	0	476
24	451	201	0	477
25	451	201	0	477
26	450	201	0	478
27	450	273	0	479
28	450	299	0	480
29	450	299	0	480
30	367	299	0	481
31	355	229	0	481
Total	10,611	4,254	5,997	

Table 10. Diversions to New York City water-supply system.—Continued
(River Master daily operation record)

[Million gallons per day for 24-hour period beginning 0800 local time]

Date 2006	East Delaware Tunnel	West Delaware Tunnel	Neversink Tunnel	Average June 1, 2005, to date
Apr. 1	341	100	0	481
2	356	224	0	482
3	352	287	0	482
4	352	300	0	483
5	0	300	0	482
6	0	300	0	481
7	251	300	0	482
8	261	300	0	482
9	302	300	0	482
10	102	300	0	482
11	0	300	0	482
12	0	297	0	481
13	271	300	0	481
14	292	300	0	482
15	133	194	0	481
16	289	300	0	481
17	289	300	0	482
18	204	420	0	482
19	196	482	0	483
20	295	308	0	483
21	295	300	0	484
22	295	300	0	484
23	296	300	0	484
24	410	12	0	484
25	453	0	0	484
26	454	0	0	484
27	57	0	0	483
28	0	0	0	481
29	441	0	0	481
30	298	0	0	480
Total	7,285	6,824	0	

Date 2006	East Delaware Tunnel	West Delaware Tunnel	Neversink Tunnel	Average June 1, 2005, to date
May 1	308	0	0	480
2	460	0	0	480
3	460	0	0	480
4	460	199	0	480
5	460	279	0	481
6	305	299	0	481
7	281	299	0	482
8	300	99	0	481
9	305	33	0	481
10	297	0	0	481
11	0	0	0	479
12	0	0	0	478
13	0	0	0	476
14	0	0	0	475
15	0	0	178	474
16	0	0	192	473
17	0	0	101	472
18	0	0	109	471
19	0	0	106	470
20	0	0	105	469
21	0	0	106	468
22	0	0	109	467
23	0	0	111	466
24	0	0	108	465
25	0	0	108	464
26	2	0	392	464
27	414	0	165	464
28	421	0	147	465
29	403	0	149	465
30	412	0	147	465
31	52	0	143	464
Total	5,340	1,208	2,476	

Table 10. Diversions to New York City water-supply system.—Continued
(River Master daily operation record)

[Million gallons per day for 24-hour period beginning 0800 local time]

Date 2006	East Delaware Tunnel	West Delaware Tunnel	Neversink Tunnel	Average June 1, 2006, to date	Date 2006	East Delaware Tunnel	West Delaware Tunnel	Neversink Tunnel	Average June 1, 2006, to date
June 1	0	0	206	206	July 1	0	0	0	312
2	0	0	197	202	2	0	0	278	311
3	443	0	197	348	3	0	0	178	307
4	445	0	195	421	4	0	0	191	303
5	445	0	197	465	5	0	0	335	304
6	451	0	143	486	6	2	0	367	306
7	458	0	101	497	7	310	0	367	316
8	61	0	102	455	8	300	0	301	323
9	0	0	91	415	9	295	0	299	330
10	0	0	106	384	10	441	0	145	337
11	0	0	158	363	11	441	0	145	343
12	0	0	274	356	12	442	0	144	349
13	87	0	150	347	13	453	0	148	354
14	103	0	145	340	14	453	0	125	360
15	6	0	149	327	15	453	0	164	365
16	313	0	153	336	16	453	0	159	371
17	399	0	145	348	17	453	0	147	375
18	399	0	144	359	18	489	0	179	382
19	429	0	146	370	19	495	0	0	384
20	448	199	0	384	20	495	0	120	389
21	448	197	0	397	21	490	0	78	392
22	452	17	111	405	22	495	0	97	396
23	152	0	90	398	23	495	0	100	400
24	0	0	95	385	24	495	0	100	403
25	299	0	96	386	25	495	0	97	407
26	17	0	0	372	26	407	0	28	407
27	0	0	0	358	27	495	0	132	411
28	0	0	0	345	28	495	0	140	415
29	0	0	0	333	29	495	0	99	418
30	0	0	0	322	30	495	0	95	421
					31	495	0	25	422
Total	5,855	413	3,391			11,327	0	4,783	

Table 10. Diversions to New York City water-supply system.—Continued
(River Master daily operation record)

[Million gallons per day for 24-hour period beginning 0800 local time]

Date 2006	East Delaware Tunnel	West Delaware Tunnel	Neversink Tunnel	Average June 1, 2006, to date
Aug. 1	495	0	143	426
2	495	10	131	429
3	495	0	274	435
4	495	0	267	440
5	495	0	246	444
6	495	0	300	449
7	495	0	306	455
8	494	0	315	460
9	494	0	357	465
10	494	0	296	470
11	493	0	299	474
12	493	0	299	479
13	493	0	299	483
14	493	0	300	487
15	492	0	301	491
16	492	0	299	495
17	492	0	304	499
18	491	0	307	503
19	491	0	307	506
20	492	0	307	510
21	492	0	303	513
22	492	0	306	517
23	492	0	316	520
24	492	263	307	527
25	491	15	303	530
26	491	0	305	533
27	491	0	305	536
28	491	0	272	539
29	491	0	325	542
30	491	0	113	542
31	492	0	0	542
Total	15,275	288	8,512	

Date 2006	East Delaware Tunnel	West Delaware Tunnel	Neversink Tunnel	Average June 1, 2006, to date
Sept. 1	492	0	0	541
2	492	0	0	541
3	492	0	0	540
4	492	0	0	540
5	492	0	0	539
6	492	0	0	539
7	492	0	0	538
8	492	0	0	538
9	492	0	0	537
10	492	0	0	537
11	492	0	0	536
12	491	0	0	536
13	491	0	0	536
14	491	0	0	535
15	491	0	0	535
16	491	0	0	534
17	491	0	0	534
18	492	0	0	534
19	492	0	0	533
20	491	0	0	533
21	491	0	0	532
22	491	0	0	532
23	491	0	0	532
24	491	0	0	531
25	497	0	0	531
26	498	0	0	531
27	493	0	1	531
28	498	0	98	531
29	497	0	110	532
30	497	0	56	532
Total	14,777	0	265	

Table 10. Diversions to New York City water-supply system.—Continued
(River Master daily operation record)

[Million gallons per day for 24-hour period beginning 0800 local time]

Date 2006	East Delaware Tunnel	West Delaware Tunnel	Neversink Tunnel	Average June 1, 2006, to date
Oct. 1	498	0	128	533
2	498	0	107	533
3	498	0	0	533
4	499	0	0	533
5	498	0	0	532
6	498	0	0	532
7	498	0	0	532
8	498	0	0	532
9	498	0	0	531
10	498	0	0	531
11	495	0	0	531
12	293	0	0	529
13	298	0	0	527
14	274	0	0	525
15	280	0	0	524
16	274	0	0	522
17	0	206	0	520
18	0	298	0	518
19	0	298	0	516
20	0	299	0	515
21	0	298	0	513
22	0	298	0	512
23	0	3	0	508
24	3	0	0	505
25	0	0	0	501
26	0	0	0	498
27	0	0	0	495
28	0	0	0	491
29	0	0	0	488
30	0	0	0	485
31	0	0	232	483
Total	6,898	1,700	467	

Date 2006	East Delaware Tunnel	West Delaware Tunnel	Neversink Tunnel	Average June 1, 2006, to date
Nov. 1	0	0	260	482
2	0	0	257	480
3	0	0	259	479
4	0	0	261	478
5	0	0	261	476
6	0	0	261	475
7	0	0	261	474
8	0	0	261	472
9	0	0	261	471
10	0	0	261	470
11	0	0	17	467
12	0	0	0	464
13	0	0	0	461
14	0	0	0	459
15	0	0	0	456
16	0	0	0	453
17	0	0	0	450
18	0	0	0	448
19	0	0	0	445
20	0	0	0	443
21	0	0	0	440
22	0	0	239	439
23	0	0	262	438
24	0	0	262	437
25	0	0	261	436
26	0	0	261	435
27	0	0	261	434
28	0	0	261	433
29	0	0	261	432
30	0	0	261	431
Total	0	0	4,949	

Table 11. Daily mean discharge, East Branch Delaware River at Downsville, New York (station number 01417000), for report year ending November 30, 2006. (U.S. Geological Survey published record)

[All values except total are in cubic feet per second, ft³/s; total in cubic feet per second days, (ft³/s)-d]

DAY	DEC	JAN	FEB	MAR	APR	MAY	JUNE	JULY	AUG	SEPT	OCT	NOV
1	43	43	1,370	181	66	388	444	2,920	156	41	84	704
2	43	43	1,330	168	56	291	746	2,210	156	41	80	705
3	41	44	1,520	168	48	141	1,000	1,740	125	41	80	705
4	42	43	1,900	167	40	65	912	1,430	132	41	80	705
5	42	42	1,930	167	33	49	737	1,230	139	41	80	705
6	42	44	2,050	168	25	60	572	1,000	150	43	80	705
7	44	58	1,890	168	16	71	473	687	156	58	80	705
8	64	74	1,740	169	16	81	857	418	157	79	80	706
9	90	74	1,700	169	16	92	1,320	257	162	93	80	705
10	92	78	1,470	164	16	95	1,610	134	167	103	86	706
11	92	82	1,230	155	16	98	1,700	47	173	119	95	707
12	101	57	1,080	156	16	69	1,620	79	178	128	95	709
13	107	43	943	139	16	109	1,430	83	181	129	99	735
14	110	44	859	86	17	168	1,330	75	181	120	109	855
15	124	43	815	47	16	263	1,580	100	182	82	112	943
16	164	267	811	39	16	448	1,420	109	182	58	125	1,090
17	163	1,320	814	39	16	670	964	109	182	50	121	2,430
18	160	4,360	422	39	28	726	562	109	182	57	92	2,400
19	150	6,680	364	40	39	795	313	122	184	63	92	2,210
20	154	4,070	363	41	34	811	211	146	149	72	93	1,880
21	160	2,840	363	41	34	819	108	152	115	92	145	1,530
22	169	2,310	560	41	30	917	77	124	93	107	178	1,310
23	175	1,930	823	45	17	873	73	115	73	115	178	1,300
24	168	1,690	822	52	25	818	153	152	91	115	178	1,300
25	160	1,620	821	53	366	740	352	152	101	105	178	1,160
26	151	1,470	821	50	844	721	2,670	172	101	90	178	1,050
27	131	1,220	818	52	931	614	7,580	175	101	92	179	952
28	111	1,050	504	62	1,110	300	15,600	159	84	93	179	654
29	60	959		67	933	168	10,100	141	59	93	501	355
30	43	971		67	510	505	4,780	89	41	93	705	558
31	43	1,170		67		211		113	41		705	
Total	3,239	34,739	30,133	3,067	5,346	12,176	61,294	14,549	4,174	2,454	5,147	31,179
Mean	104	1,121	1,076	98.9	178	393	2,043	469	135	81.8	166	1,039

Year total 207,497 (ft³/s)-d

Mean 568 ft³/s

Table 12. Daily mean discharge, West Branch Delaware River at Stilesville, New York (station number 01425000), for report year ending November 30, 2006. (U.S. Geological Survey published record)

[All values except total are in cubic feet per second, ft³/s; total in cubic feet per second days, (ft³/s)-d]

DAY	DEC	JAN	FEB	MAR	APR	MAY	JUNE	JULY	AUG	SEPT	OCT	NOV
1	57	55	1,680	360	162	1,280	680	6,040	839	569	1,020	2,240
2	54	50	1,740	355	225	1,120	678	4,150	823	790	1,020	2,120
3	52	54	1,900	340	216	990	813	3,310	656	849	1,020	2,060
4	52	56	2,430	334	204	865	1,050	2,720	492	860	1,030	2,010
5	52	57	2,730	324	231	643	1,120	2,020	389	825	1,050	1,790
6	51	57	2,790	318	244	453	1,090	1,480	420	768	1,050	1,560
7	48	57	2,550	311	257	334	1,030	1,160	441	696	1,030	1,370
8	52	57	2,220	289	316	260	1,000	1,080	475	621	1,020	1,270
9	75	57	1,890	270	363	267	1,060	1,010	415	556	1,020	1,370
10	79	107	1,650	280	372	294	1,170	745	370	509	1,020	1,430
11	80	279	1,440	272	368	316	1,290	542	632	465	1,010	1,370
12	81	713	1,280	260	349	393	1,350	631	812	413	507	1,320
13	90	1,290	1,140	238	328	464	1,340	847	670	381	1,010	1,300
14	96	2,090	1,030	354	326	459	1,230	953	677	396	1,010	1,270
15	98	4,080	936	824	367	446	1,230	1,040	729	693	1,020	1,230
16	122	4,030	872	1,140	390	442	1,260	945	680	907	1,010	1,360
17	126	3,400	836	1,250	345	449	1,210	845	726	916	1,020	3,450
18	120	3,930	832	1,230	294	474	1,110	763	906	858	1,020	3,920
19	102	6,530	740	1,150	205	493	887	603	717	796	1,020	3,430
20	91	5,690	650	1,060	134	515	663	399	674	728	1,030	2,850
21	114	4,460	608	865	117	537	467	371	432	652	1,020	2,320
22	188	3,530	581	723	119	595	413	337	486	824	1,020	1,980
23	203	2,850	559	611	612	644	496	257	581	1,230	1,010	1,960
24	196	2,350	532	512	2,350	637	588	335	785	1,080	1,020	2,050
25	170	1,950	496	449	3,250	622	592	368	882	1,000	1,010	1,930
26	144	1,670	456	414	3,120	599	1,060	399	718	992	1,020	1,790
27	111	1,420	412	381	2,670	598	7,440	370	541	1,020	1,010	1,540
28	83	1,250	378	317	2,200	581	27,700	400	265	1,010	1,020	1,370
29	59	1,140		256	1,780	541	18,300	531	184	1,020	1,870	1,250
30	59	1,130		206	1,500	608	9,640	637	100	1,020	2,880	1,150
31	57	1,310		165		666		787	256		2,710	
Total	2,962	55,699	35,358	15,858	23,414	17,585	87,957	36,075	17,773	23,444	35,527	56,060
Mean	95.5	1,797	1,263	512	780	567	2,932	1,164	573	781	1,146	1,869

Year total 407,712 (ft³/s)-d

Mean 1,117 ft³/s

51

Table 13. Daily mean discharge, Neversink River at Neversink, New York (station number 01436000), for report year ending November 30, 2006.

[All values except total are in cubic feet per second, ft³/s; total in cubic feet per second days, (ft³/s)-d]

DAY	DEC	JAN	FEB	MAR	APR	MAY	JUNE	JULY	AUG	SEPT	OCT	NOV
1	28	27	346	110	87	58	41	541	182	24	64	185
2	28	27	273	126	57	60	41	329	177	24	61	184
3	28	28	487	120	55	56	41	89	118	24	61	184
4	28	28	724	116	47	63	41	82	112	24	60	183
5	28	28	976	117	31	77	41	50	113	24	61	183
6	28	27	743	121	28	89	35	25	114	24	63	183
7	28	27	498	123	22	89	26	37	114	24	63	185
8	28	27	387	123	22	98	26	64	111	35	63	172
9	28	27	277	123	22	102	28	80	108	53	63	55
10	28	27	168	117	39	103	129	83	110	62	67	130
11	28	28	188	106	52	103	111	63	114	69	74	183
12	28	29	173	112	53	62	59	72	119	75	68	183
13	28	28	136	92	60	50	50	79	123	76	63	183
14	28	29	134	43	58	51	49	88	123	69	63	183
15	28	61	169	28	44	122	53	114	118	32	65	183
16	29	260	164	33	49	199	62	123	117	24	65	169
17	28	399	109	37	59	481	92	123	117	24	66	419
18	28	2,530	33	38	73	316	117	123	117	24	65	722
19	34	2,010	46	38	79	281	93	109	118	24	65	528
20	57	888	53	46	79	320	76	100	115	23	66	421
21	73	627	53	51	88	258	65	101	111	25	65	369
22	75	474	53	53	73	203	73	81	112	45	65	287
23	81	434	53	53	43	137	79	45	115	47	65	168
24	81	391	50	62	47	102	79	79	145	47	66	183
25	79	436	50	66	54	132	80	87	112	60	67	183
26	67	382	49	64	55	60	1,330	112	111	67	67	183
27	39	281	60	61	56	40	2,550	112	112	67	79	183
28	27	258	93	75	57	40	4,740	104	93	67	57	181
29	28	244		84	57	61	1,900	97	59	69	59	179
30	26	266		84	57	101	853	95	35	69	183	179
31	27	343		86		63		127	24		183	
Total	1,199	10,671	6,545	2,508	1,603	3,977	12,960	3,414	3,469	1,321	2,242	6,913
Mean	38.7	344	234	80.9	53.4	128	432	110	112	44.0	72.3	230

Year total 56,822 (ft³/s)-d

Mean 156 ft³/s

52

Table 14. Daily mean discharge, Delaware River at Mortague, New Jersey (station number 01438500), for report year ending November 30, 2006. (U.S. Geological Survey published record)

[All values except total are in cubic feet per second, ft³/s; total in cubic feet per second days, (ft³/s)-d; e, estimated]

DAY	DEC	JAN	FEB	MAR	APR	MAY	JUNE	JULY	AUG	SEPT	OCT	NOV
1	22,100	11,200	15,000	e3,900	2,390	6,520	7,150	38,600	3,160	6,970	7,940	12,400
2	14,700	9,270	13,900	3,510	2,220	5,690	6,530	26,100	2,930	6,210	7,630	11,700
3	11,800	9,600	14,100	3,380	2,350	5,120	5,280	19,900	2,920	5,890	7,110	11,900
4	9,720	9,410	21,000	e3,390	2,740	4,650	7,420	16,400	2,670	5,070	6,350	10,000
5	8,480	8,160	22,900	2,520	3,180	4,160	7,840	13,600	2,430	4,210	5,920	8,920
6	7,620	8,140	22,400	2,870	3,220	3,500	7,290	11,200	1,810	4,370	5,600	8,170
7	6,780	7,530	18,200	3,240	3,040	3,100	6,370	9,370	1,690	4,020	5,100	7,490
8	6,040	6,510	15,600	3,040	3,030	2,890	8,370	8,280	2,030	3,880	4,620	8,010
9	5,420	6,050	13,300	2,930	3,290	3,200	8,640	7,550	1,980	3,570	4,230	15,900
10	4,480	5,810	11,600	3,010	3,200	3,090	7,460	6,920	1,870	3,370	3,850	13,800
11	4,370	5,840	10,400	3,290	3,000	3,560	7,240	5,800	1,710	3,100	3,700	11,400
12	4,350	8,560	9,330	2,920	2,920	5,760	7,180	4,830	1,870	3,000	3,830	10,200
13	4,160	11,800	8,470	3,040	2,880	6,660	7,100	4,640	1,570	2,870	3,760	9,490
14	3,690	14,700	7,840	4,370	2,830	6,720	6,640	4,770	1,720	2,790	3,450	9,260
15	3,610	33,400	7,390	5,370	3,030	6,210	6,280	4,130	1,920	7,820	3,260	9,160
16	4,550	23,900	7,050	4,830	3,520	7,170	6,400	3,930	2,050	14,600	3,110	8,460
17	6,530	19,400	7,100	4,500	3,220	9,190	5,540	3,860	2,010	10,300	3,240	29,200
18	6,510	28,200	6,860	4,370	2,970	8,850	4,770	3,540	1,960	7,870	5,280	28,900
19	5,110	58,500	6,000	3,860	2,700	8,130	4,370	3,300	2,010	6,700	6,770	21,400
20	e4,700	39,400	4,890	3,690	2,500	8,290	4,130	3,140	1,890	6,080	6,140	17,500
21	e5,000	28,800	4,850	3,790	2,360	7,350	3,890	3,080	2,920	5,610	14,000	14,600
22	5,090	23,200	4,610	3,460	2,300	6,640	3,550	3,260	2,870	5,030	11,800	12,200
23	4,570	19,700	4,560	3,250	6,650	6,350	3,320	3,590	2,110	4,590	9,090	11,900
24	4,150	17,500	4,630	3,030	17,100	5,790	3,020	3,240	1,860	4,820	7,560	14,800
25	4,060	15,400	4,430	2,800	17,800	5,310	2,910	3,180	1,800	4,820	6,550	12,800
26	6,180	13,300	3,660	2,790	14,600	5,080	12,300	3,090	2,080	4,530	5,920	11,300
27	9,150	11,800	3,660	2,830	12,500	5,470	58,400	2,880	2,370	4,230	5,450	10,400
28	8,270	10,700	3,800	2,880	10,200	5,120	161,000	2,910	3,010	4,090	10,000	9,550
29	7,520	10,200		2,770	8,670	4,500	156,000	2,880	4,280	6,790	29,600	8,800
30	12,800	10,200		2,710	7,490	3,860	67,400	2,540	10,200	10,300	19,300	7,910
31	13,900	11,700		2,470		4,880		2,730	9,870		15,000	
Total	225,410	497,880	277,530	104,810	157,900	172,810	603,790	233,240	85,570	167,500	235,160	377,520
Mean	7,271	16,060	9,912	3,381	5,263	5,575	20,130	7,524	2,760	5,583	7,586	12,580

Year total 3,139,120 (ft³/s)-d

Mean 8,600 ft³/s

Table 15. Diversions by New Jersey; daily mean discharge, Delaware and Raritan Canal at Port Mercer, New Jersey (station number 01460440), for report year ending November 30, 2006.

(U.S. Geological Survey published record)

[All data except total are in million gallons per day, Mgal/d; total in million gallons, Mgal; e, estimated]

DAY	DEC	JAN	FEB	MAR	APR	MAY	JUNE	JULY	AUG	SEPT	OCT	NOV
1	87	97	91	100	97	99	100	101	101	89	96	96
2	85	97	91	102	97	98	87	100	105	85	95	96
3	83	49	91	99	94	99	66	100	e100	68	95	87
4	88	81	90	95	94	100	86	103	e98	88	96	86
5	90	90	83	95	94	100	98	102	e97	93	91	92
6	92	88	87	95	97	101	98	97	e98	90	92	95
7	90	89	93	98	96	101	93	95	e97	93	94	97
8	89	87	97	95	95	101	97	98	99	94	95	12
9	92	91	98	97	92	101	92	102	98	94	95	22
10	93	90	96	96	96	101	97	100	98	94	97	84
11	95	91	98	98	98	99	96	102	96	92	91	86
12	98	86	102	98	97	96	99	100	96	92	65	89
13	102	88	e101	94	97	92	99	100	95	93	81	85
14	e99	80	103	93	96	94	96	100	96	92	88	79
15	e110	75	101	92	97	95	94	101	99	92	90	89
16	e78	85	99	94	95	75	95	99	101	91	92	84
17	84	90	95	96	93	85	96	98	97	94	83	84
18	93	67	94	95	95	92	98	97	98	94	80	82
19	97	66	95	94	98	95	e100	95	96	96	91	73
20	98	88	96	95	100	93	101	95	97	95	88	77
21	98	90	97	94	98	94	98	98	97	95	82	93
22	98	95	96	94	99	95	98	90	100	94	83	94
23	98	75	96	95	73	96	100	96	96	96	86	76
24	99	85	99	94	87	96	99	99	97	97	85	63
25	99	86	98	94	91	98	86	98	94	97	86	70
26	94	89	99	94	95	99	102	100	100	97	86	78
27	97	89	98	93	97	99	102	100	91	99	85	70
28	99	90	100	93	100	99	78	102	95	100	44	77
29	98	91		101	97	97	90	96	95	99	69	83
30	96	92		100	98	97	92	100	91	97	83	84
31	97	93		96		97		100	89		87	
Total	2,916	2,650	2,684	2,969	2,853	2,984	2,833	3,064	3,007	2,790	2,671	2,383
Mean	94.1	85.5	95.9	95.8	95.1	96.3	94.4	98.8	97.0	93.0	86.2	79.4

Year total 33,804 Mgal

Mean 92.6 Mgal/d

QUALITY OF WATER IN THE DELAWARE ESTUARY

Introduction

This section describes the water-quality monitoring program for the Delaware Estuary during the River Master 2006 report year, December 1, 2005, to November 30, 2006. This program is conducted by the USGS, in cooperation with the DRBC. Selected data collected for this program are presented and water-quality conditions are summarized. The DRBC and others use these data to assess water-quality conditions and track the movement of the "salt front" in the Delaware Estuary.

Water-Quality Monitoring Program

As part of a long-term program, the quality of water in the Delaware Estuary between Trenton, New Jersey, and Reedy Island Jetty, Delaware, is monitored at various locations (fig. 6). Data on water temperature, specific conductance, dissolved oxygen, and pH were collected by electronic instruments at four sites—Trenton, Benjamin Franklin Bridge (Philadelphia), Chester, and Reedy Island Jetty. Water-quality monitors at Trenton and Reedy Island Jetty were operated continuously throughout the report year, whereas monitors at the Benjamin Franklin Bridge and Chester were operated from April to November 2006.

The frequency of water-quality sampling was monthly in March, June, July, and October, and twice monthly in April, May, August, and September 2006. Water samples at 19 sites between Biles Channel and Mahon River (sample sites A–T on fig. 6) were collected and analyzed by the State of Delaware for the DRBC. At each of these sites, water samples were collected near the center of the channel at a depth of 3 feet below the water surface and analyzed for selected physical properties and chemical constituents including, but not limited to, water temperature, chloride, alkalinity, specific conductance, dissolved oxygen, pH, selected nutrients, and trace metals. These analyses consist of field measurements and laboratory determinations.

From March to October, but excluding June, water-quality samples were collected on a once-monthly basis at three additional sites in the lower Delaware Bay (sites U–W on fig. 6) and analyzed for selected physical properties and chemical constituents.

Data obtained from the electronic water-quality monitors are processed and stored in the USGS National Water Information System database. These data are published annually by the USGS in water resources data reports for New Jersey and Pennsylvania. Water-quality data for the other sampling sites are not presented in this report but are available from DRBC and STORET, an environmental quality database operated by the U.S. Environmental Protection Agency.

Water Quality During the 2006 Report Year

Streamflow

Streamflow has a major effect on the quality of water in the Delaware Estuary. High freshwater inflows commonly result in improved water quality by limiting the upstream movement of seawater and reducing the concentration of dissolved substances. High inflows also aid in maintaining lower water

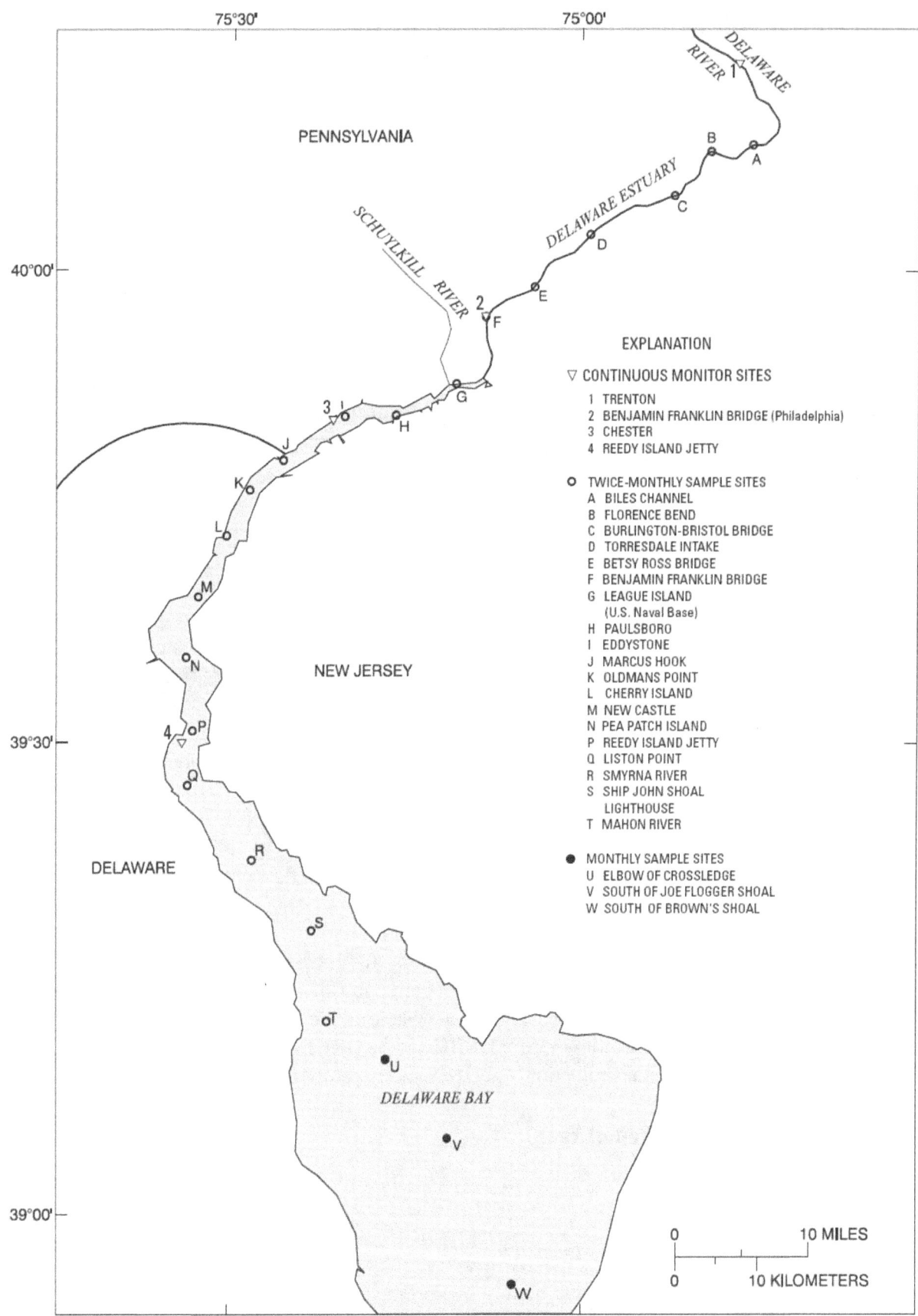

EXPLANATION

▽ CONTINUOUS MONITOR SITES

1 TRENTON
2 BENJAMIN FRANKLIN BRIDGE (Philadelphia)
3 CHESTER
4 REEDY ISLAND JETTY

○ TWICE-MONTHLY SAMPLE SITES

A BILES CHANNEL
B FLORENCE BEND
C BURLINGTON-BRISTOL BRIDGE
D TORRESDALE INTAKE
E BETSY ROSS BRIDGE
F BENJAMIN FRANKLIN BRIDGE
G LEAGUE ISLAND
  (U.S. Naval Base)
H PAULSBORO
I EDDYSTONE
J MARCUS HOOK
K OLDMANS POINT
L CHERRY ISLAND
M NEW CASTLE
N PEA PATCH ISLAND
P REEDY ISLAND JETTY
Q LISTON POINT
R SMYRNA RIVER
S SHIP JOHN SHOAL
  LIGHTHOUSE
T MAHON RIVER

● MONTHLY SAMPLE SITES

U ELBOW OF CROSSLEDGE
V SOUTH OF JOE FLOGGER SHOAL
W SOUTH OF BROWN'S SHOAL

Figure 6. Location of water-quality monitoring sites on the Delaware Estuary.

temperatures during warm weather and in supporting higher concentrations of dissolved oxygen. Under certain conditions, however, high streamflows can transport large quantities of nutrients to the estuary, which may result in excessive levels of algae.

Streamflow from the Delaware River Basin upstream of Trenton, New Jersey, is the major source of freshwater inflow to the Delaware Estuary. During the report year, monthly mean streamflow measured at the USGS gaging station Delaware River at Trenton, New Jersey, was highest during January 2006 (31,770 ft^3/s) and lowest during August 2006 (5,644 ft^3/s; table 16)[2]. Monthly mean streamflows were less than long-term mean monthly flows in March, April, May, and August and greater than the long-term flows in the other eight months. The greatest flow deficiency was in March 2006, when monthly mean streamflow was 38 percent of the long-term mean monthly flow. Long-term monthly mean streamflow was computed on the basis of data for the period from 1913 to 2005. The highest daily mean streamflow during the report year was 224,000 ft^3/s on June 29, 2006. The lowest daily mean streamflow was 3,850 ft^3/s on August 15, 2006.

Water Temperature

Water temperature has an important influence on water quality, as it affects various physical, chemical, and biological properties of water. Generally, increases in water temperature have detrimental effects on water quality by decreasing the saturation level of dissolved oxygen and increasing the biological activity of aquatic organisms. Although the primary factors that affect water temperature in the Delaware Estuary are climatic, various kinds of water use, especially powerplant cooling, also can have significant effects.

At the Benjamin Franklin Bridge, Philadelphia, Pennsylvania, water-temperature data were collected continuously from April to November 2006. Monthly mean temperatures were greater than the long-term mean monthly temperatures in April, May, and August 2006 and were less than the long-term means in June, July, and from September to November 2006. Long-term mean water temperatures were computed using data for the period from 1964 to 2005 (fig. 7). The maximum daily mean water temperature of 29.1°C was recorded on August 4 and 5, 2006.

Specific Conductance and Chloride

Specific conductance is a measure of the capacity of water to conduct an electrical current and is a function of the types and quantities of dissolved substances in water. As concentrations of dissolved ions increase, specific conductance of the water also increases. Specific conductance measurements are good indicators of dissolved solids content and total ion concentrations. Seawater and some man-made constituents can cause the specific conductance of estuary water to increase substantially. Dilution associated with high freshwater inflows results in decreased levels of dissolved solids and lower specific conductance whereas low inflows have the opposite effect.

The upstream movement of seawater and the accompanying increase in chloride concentrations is an important concern for water supplies obtained from the Delaware Estuary. Water with chloride concentrations greater than 250 milligrams per liter (mg/L) is considered undesirable for domestic use, and water with concentrations exceeding 50 mg/L is unsatisfactory for chemically sensitive consumers and some

---

[2]All numbered tables in the section "Quality of Water in the Delaware Estuary" are grouped at the end of this section, beginning on page 62.

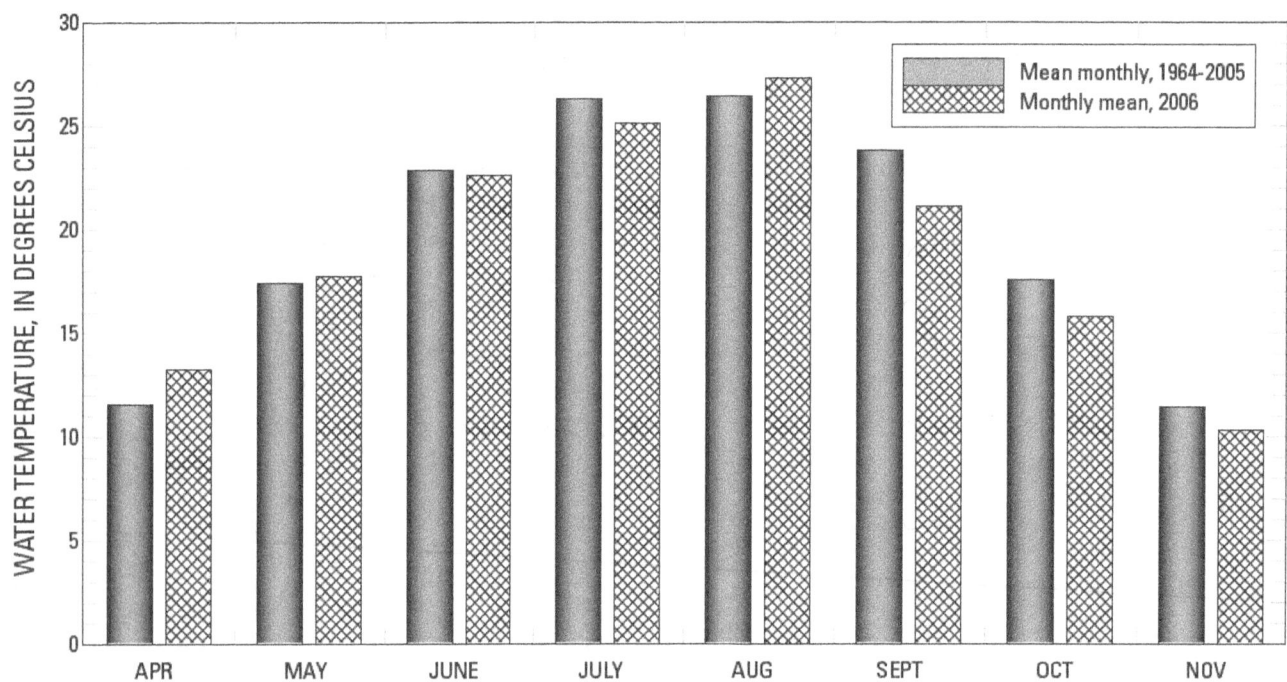

Figure 7. Water temperature in the Delaware Estuary at Benjamin Franklin Bridge at Philadelphia, Pennsylvania, April to November.

industrial processes. Chloride concentrations in the estuary increase in a downstream direction, with increasing proximity to the Atlantic Ocean.

Chloride concentration was not measured directly at the monitor site at Reedy Island Jetty, Delaware. Rather, a mathematical relation between specific conductance and chloride concentration has been developed on the basis of long-term field measurements of specific conductance and laboratory analyses of chloride; this relation was used to estimate chloride concentrations from specific conductance values. Chloride concentrations estimated from the relation are presented in table 17. The specific conductance-chloride relation is less reliable when chloride concentrations are less than 30 mg/L, because other chemical substances may be present in quantities large enough to affect the relation. Thus, chloride concentrations estimated from specific conductance data are not presented when concentrations of less than 30 mg/L result from the relation. Instead, estimated values less than 30 mg/L are reported as < 30 mg/L. Chloride concentrations at Chester, Pennsylvania (table 18), were measured directly by Kimberly Clark Chester Operations and are not derived from specific conductance data.

At Chester, the greatest daily maximum chloride concentration was 120 mg/L on August 26–28, 2006 (table 18). During the report year, daily maximum concentrations exceeded 50 mg/L on 27 percent of the days. The lowest daily minimum chloride concentration was 18 mg/L on July 1, 2006. Daily minimum concentrations exceeded 50 mg/L on 17 percent of the days. Chloride concentrations were persistently high from December 19–31, 2005, from April 3–25, 2006, and from August 15 to September 1, 2006, when daily minimum concentrations exceeded 50 mg/L on most days.

At Reedy Island Jetty, the greatest daily maximum chloride concentration was 7,100 mg/L on September 2, 2006 (table 17). Daily maximum chloride concentrations during the report year exceeded 1,000 mg/L on 93 percent of the days. The lowest daily minimum chloride concentration was <30 mg/L on several days in each of the following months: January, June, and July 2006. Daily minimum chloride concentrations exceeded 1,000 mg/L on 52 percent of the days. From December to May, daily maximum chloride concentrations at Reedy Island Jetty ranged from 33 to 6,900 mg/L. From June to November, daily maximum chloride concentrations ranged from 45 to 7,100 mg/L.

Dissolved Oxygen

Dissolved oxygen in water is necessary for the respiratory processes of aquatic organisms and for chemical reactions in aquatic environments. Fish and many other clean-water species require relatively high dissolved-oxygen concentrations at all times. The major source of dissolved oxygen in the Delaware Estuary is diffusion from the atmosphere, and, to a lesser extent, photosynthetic activity of aquatic plants. The principal factors that affect dissolved-oxygen concentrations in the estuary are water temperature, bio-chemical oxygen demand, freshwater inflow, phytoplankton, turbidity, salinity, and tidal and wind-driven mixing.

Concentrations of dissolved oxygen at several sites on the Delaware Estuary have been measured since 1962 by the USGS. Two of these sites, Delaware River at Benjamin Franklin Bridge at Philadelphia, Pennsylvania, and Delaware River at Chester, Pennsylvania, have nearly continuous records and are in the reach of the estuary most affected by effluent discharges. The mean, and minimum daily mean, dissolved-oxygen concentrations from July to September at these station during the 1965–2006 report years are shown in figure 8. Although concentrations have increased considerably over this 42-year period, mean concentrations can vary considerably from year to year.

Concentrations of dissolved oxygen in the Delaware Estuary generally are greatest near Trenton and decrease in a downstream direction. In an area just downstream of the Benjamin Franklin Bridge, concentrations commonly reach minimum levels. During the report year, daily mean concentrations of dissolved oxygen at the Benjamin Franklin Bridge monitor site were lowest in late August, and the lowest recorded daily mean concentration was 3.7 mg/L on August 30 (table 19). Daily mean concentrations of dissolved oxygen were consistently 6.0 mg/L or greater on all days from April 1 to June 3; June 30 to July 15; September 3–6; and September 18 to November 30, 2006. At Chester, daily mean dissolved-oxygen concentrations were lowest during mid- to late June, late July, and early August, and the lowest recorded daily mean concentration was 4.6 mg/L on various dates in June, July, and August 2006 (table 20).

Histograms of hourly dissolved-oxygen concentrations at the Benjamin Franklin Bridge and Chester monitor sites during the critical summer period—July to September 2006—are presented in figure 9. Hourly concentrations at the Benjamin Franklin Bridge were 4 mg/L or less during about 18 percent of this period. At Chester, hourly dissolved-oxygen concentrations were 4 mg/L or less during 0.64 percent of the 2006 critical summer period. Dissolved-oxygen concentrations less than 4 mg/L can have adverse, and possibly lethal, effects on fish and other aquatic organisms.

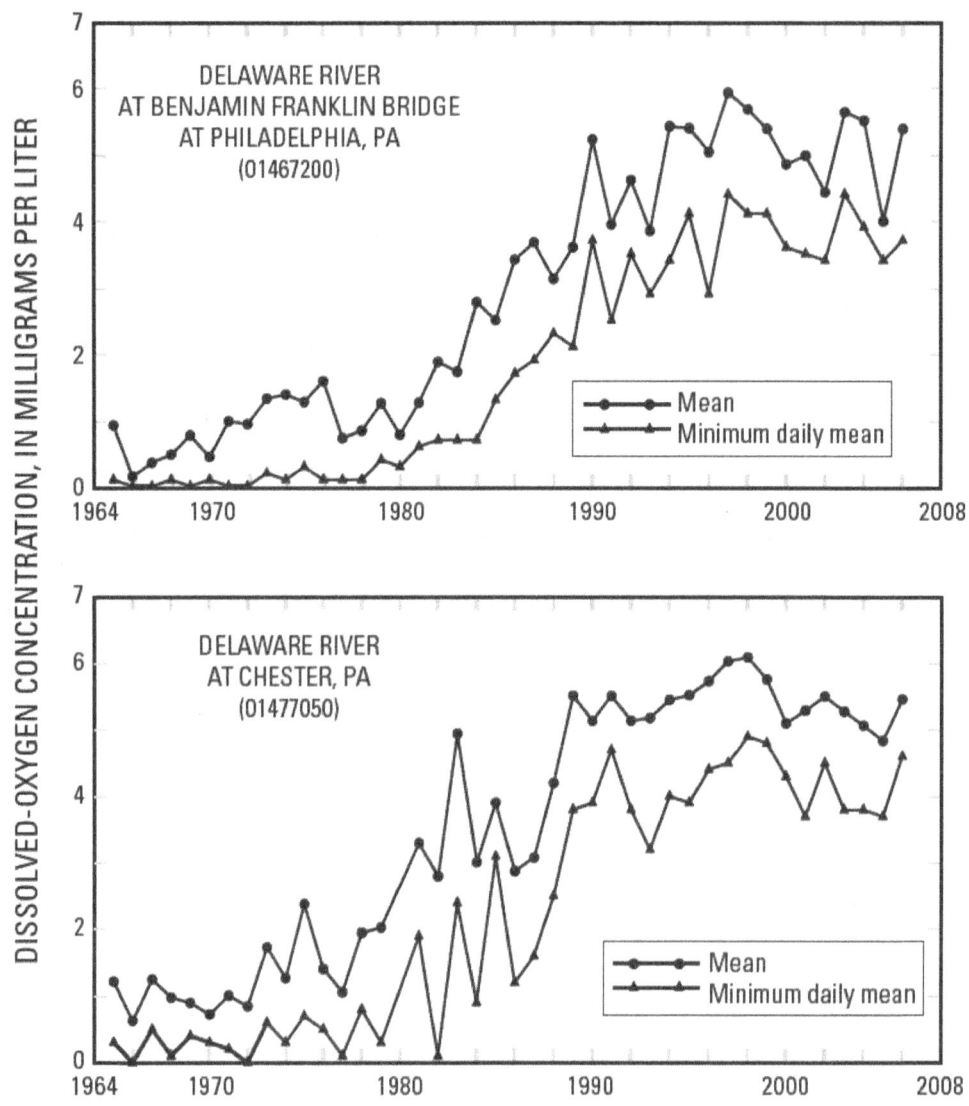

Figure 8. Mean and minimum daily mean dissolved-oxygen concentrations from July to September at two monitor sites on the Delaware Estuary, 1965–2006.

Hydrogen-Ion Activity (pH)

The pH of a solution is a measure of the effective concentration (activity) of dissolved hydrogen ions. Solutions having pH less than 7 are characterized as acidic, whereas solutions with pH greater than 7 are considered basic or alkaline. The pH of uncontaminated surface water generally ranges from 6.5 to 8.5. Major factors affecting the pH of surface water include the geologic composition of the drainage basin and human inputs, including effluent discharges. In addition, photosynthetic activity, and dissolved gases including carbon dioxide, hydrogen sulfide, and ammonia can have a considerable effect on pH. During the report year, pH was measured seasonally at the Benjamin Franklin Bridge and Chester monitor sites, and continuously at the Reedy Island Jetty site. During these periods, the ranges of daily median pH measured at these stations were as follows: Benjamin Franklin Bridge, 6.3 to 7.6; Chester, 6.9 to 7.5; and Reedy Island Jetty, 6.9 to 8.2. Generally, the pH of water in the Delaware Estuary is lowest near Trenton, New Jersey, and increases (that is, water becomes more alkaline) in a downstream direction. The pH of water in the Delaware Estuary between the Benjamin Franklin Bridge and Reedy Island Jetty is not a limiting factor for aquatic health or other beneficial uses of the water.

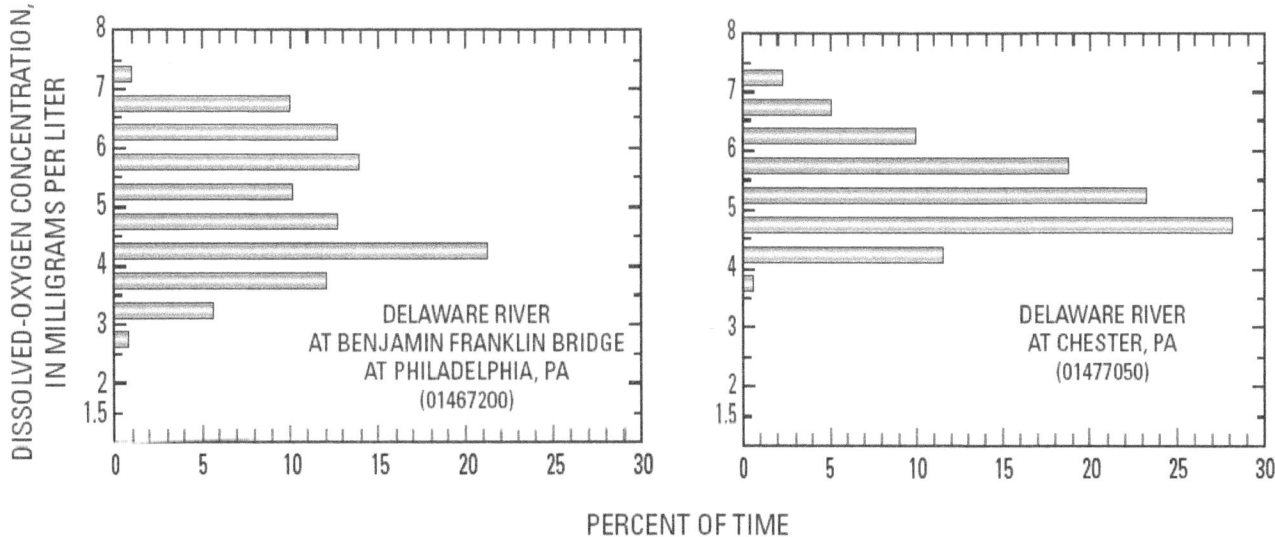

Figure 9. Distribution of hourly dissolved-oxygen concentrations at two monitor sites on the Delaware Estuary, July to September 2006.

Table 16. Daily mean discharge, Delaware River at Trenton, New Jersey (station number 01463500), for report year ending November 30, 2006. (U.S. Geological Survey published record)

[All values, except total, are in cubic feet per second; total in cubic feet per second days, (ft³/s)-d; e, estimated]

DAY	DEC	JAN	FEB	MAR	APR	MAY	JUNE	JULY	AUG	SEPT	OCT	NOV
1	37,100	25,300	23,100	8,790	5,780	14,100	7,720	89,800	7,350	17,800	15,800	26,600
2	36,500	22,000	25,400	8,810	5,600	12,600	13,000	60,600	7,270	17,100	13,600	23,100
3	27,300	31,800	25,500	9,040	5,450	11,400	21,200	45,700	6,730	17,400	13,000	22,800
4	22,700	32,700	32,400	8,060	5,430	10,500	14,000	36,400	6,480	14,800	12,300	21,500
5	19,800	27,400	40,600	7,910	6,000	9,760	13,400	34,300	6,270	12,200	13,800	18,400
6	17,400	23,300	41,200	7,580	6,590	9,070	13,600	33,700	5,790	10,200	14,600	16,700
7	15,800	21,100	36,900	7,350	6,810	8,300	13,100	29,300	5,380	9,450	12,400	15,700
8	14,400	18,900	32,000	7,860	6,990	7,460	13,500	23,000	4,820	9,180	11,200	25,600
9	13,300	17,000	28,300	7,560	9,020	6,920	14,700	17,600	4,540	8,350	10,300	33,200
10	12,600	16,000	24,800	7,500	8,590	6,920	14,500	18,300	4,620	7,790	9,640	32,600
11	11,400	15,300	21,900	7,460	7,900	6,860	12,800	16,600	4,550	7,350	9,270	27,400
12	10,800	17,200	20,500	7,810	7,300	8,180	11,900	14,900	4,360	6,800	9,640	23,200
13	10,400	19,700	18,900	7,730	6,950	12,800	11,500	14,800	4,100	6,290	9,180	21,100
14	10,000	25,200	17,400	7,790	6,810	14,000	11,200	13,300	4,140	6,430	9,000	20,800
15	8,930	36,300	16,500	8,670	6,760	13,900	10,600	11,800	3,850	11,700	8,300	19,200
16	15,900	47,600	16,100	e9,800	6,960	14,500	9,870	12,000	4,320	23,300	8,040	19,000
17	22,800	35,700	17,600	e9,500	7,080	16,100	9,780	10,600	4,530	27,200	8,220	31,600
18	19,200	37,300	17,200	9,000	7,130	16,700	9,140	9,500	4,380	20,400	11,500	51,900
19	17,400	74,400	15,400	8,770	6,610	15,800	8,060	9,260	4,220	16,900	12,900	44,300
20	15,300	82,000	13,800	8,160	6,220	14,900	8,380	8,610	4,190	15,100	15,000	36,300
21	13,200	59,000	12,200	7,590	5,720	14,600	7,560	7,860	4,440	13,500	15,000	31,500
22	11,900	46,200	11,800	7,610	5,870	13,500	6,950	14,100	4,230	12,400	20,600	27,700
23	11,600	41,700	11,600	7,330	13,700	12,200	6,580	12,500	5,250	11,000	18,900	25,800
24	11,500	38,700	11,200	6,970	20,300	11,500	7,490	10,400	4,670	9,850	16,100	32,800
25	11,200	32,900	10,900	6,790	31,100	10,800	9,060	9,270	4,070	9,500	14,000	30,600
26	15,500	28,700	10,500	6,590	28,600	10,100	11,100	8,330	4,310	9,300	12,400	26,900
27	19,300	25,500	9,370	6,500	24,300	9,720	53,500	7,750	4,740	9,090	11,500	24,100
28	21,100	22,800	8,620	6,390	20,800	10,100	154,000	8,400	6,110	8,630	20,000	21,800
29	19,800	21,000		6,330	17,500	9,580	224,000	8,430	8,370	9,040	36,400	20,200
30	20,400	21,100		6,240	15,600	8,790	179,000	8,290	9,870	11,300	43,700	18,700
31	25,700	21,200		6,090		7,690		7,470	17,000		33,000	
Total	540,230	985,000	571,690	239,580	319,470	349,350	901,190	612,870	174,950	369,350	469,290	791,100
Mean	17,430	31,770	20,420	7,728	10,650	11,270	30,040	19,770	5,644	12,310	15,140	26,370

Year total 6,324,070 (ft³/s)-d

Mean 17,330 ft³/s

Table 17. Daily maximum and minimum chloride concentrations estimated from values of specific conductance, Delaware River at Reedy Island Jetty, Delaware (station number 01482800), for report year ending November 30, 2006.

[Concentrations in milligrams per liter; ---, missing data; Max, maximum value; Min, minimum value; <, less than; n.d., not determined]

DAY	DEC Max	DEC Min	JAN Max	JAN Min	FEB Max	FEB Min	MAR Max	MAR Min	APR Max	APR Min	MAY Max	MAY Min	JUNE Max	JUNE Min	JULY Max	JULY Min	AUG Max	AUG Min	SEPT Max	SEPT Min	OCT Max	OCT Min	NOV Max	NOV Min
1	3,400	810	2,500	470	2,600	460	3,600	900	5,400	2,900	4,300	1,500	4,600	2,000	49	<30	3,100	760	6,100	3,000	4,100	1,400	3,000	140
2	2,200	470	1,900	420	2,200	510	3,900	980	4,700	2,700	4,800	1,500	4,100	2,000	45	<30	3,400	810	7,100	3,600	4,200	1,300	3,000	300
3	950	110	1,700	110	1,600	470	3,400	1,000	5,000	2,700	3,400	1,300	4,100	1,800	48	32	4,100	920	5,500	2,500	4,400	1,200	2,600	290
4	1,700	120	1,800	190	1,000	400	2,500	890	4,700	2,700	4,200	1,400	4,000	1,400	460	<30	5,000	950	4,000	2,200	4,300	1,200	2,600	270
5	1,600	120	1,300	210	1,300	290	3,700	890	5,200	2,600	4,200	1,500	4,600	1,300	880	32	5,800	1,500	4,400	2,000	4,700	1,200	2,800	340
6	1,800	160	590	180	410	150	4,400	1,200	5,000	2,600	4,600	1,700	4,700	1,800	1,900	37	6,800	2,200	4,500	1,800	4,700	1,500	2,900	420
7	840	150	750	160	310	100	4,500	1,500	5,800	2,900	4,800	1,900	6,100	2,400	2,000	86	6,700	1,900	4,600	1,800	5,400	1,900	2,600	400
8	1,700	130	740	130	940	61	4,600	1,700	5,500	2,700	4,700	2,500	5,700	2,100	2,800	140	6,700	1,400	5,200	1,900	4,700	1,900	2,900	450
9	2,600	170	1,100	160	1,900	60	4,800	2,000	6,500	3,000	6,100	2,600	5,700	1,900	2,800	290	5,800	2,600	5,100	1,900	4,500	1,900	2,000	240
10	2,500	190	930	150	2,400	83	5,500	2,000	6,400	2,900	6,800	2,700	5,700	2,100	2,500	280	7,000	1,900	4,800	1,800	4,500	1,800	910	150
11	3,000	380	1,100	150	2,500	170	4,500	1,500	6,300	2,900	6,800	2,800	5,800	2,000	2,300	290	6,000	2,300	5,400	2,100	5,300	1,800	1,200	150
12	2,900	460	900	130	3,600	530	4,400	1,500	5,800	3,000	6,900	3,000	6,000	1,600	1,900	280	6,200	2,600	5,400	2,200	4,600	2,000	1,500	140
13	2,900	500	920	130	4,100	700	4,700	1,800	5,200	2,700	6,300	2,900	5,800	1,700	1,900	290	5,800	2,000	5,100	2,300	4,400	1,700	3,200	150
14	3,300	490	1,400	150	2,600	570	4,000	1,900	5,600	2,700	6,200	2,700	5,400	1,900	1,900	310	5,900	2,900	4,800	2,400	4,300	1,800	3,500	780
15	3,400	800	740	44	2,100	550	2,900	990	5,800	3,000	5,300	2,600	5,200	2,000	2,000	330	5,200	1,800	4,100	2,000	4,500	1,700	3,200	570
16	3,300	680	2,400	150	2,200	520	3,200	900	6,100	2,900	5,400	2,500	5,400	2,000	1,500	330	6,000	1,800	4,600	2,000	4,900	1,500	3,200	700
17	1,700	400	2,000	250	2,200	460	4,000	1,100	5,800	2,900	5,300	2,300	5,100	2,100	1,900	360	5,800	1,600	4,900	1,500	5,200	1,900	1,900	320
18	1,600	370	1,800	92	990	330	3,300	1,400	5,700	2,600	5,500	2,200	4,800	1,900	2,200	420	5,800	2,400	4,600	1,400	4,300	2,000	1,500	140
19	1,700	350	250	42	1,300	240	3,700	1,300	5,700	3,000	5,100	2,200	4,000	1,700	2,300	410	6,200	2,000	4,600	1,500	4,300	1,600	1,300	96
20	1,600	290	56	34	2,100	250	4,400	1,500	5,700	2,800	4,800	2,100	4,500	1,600	2,800	430	5,600	1,700	4,600	1,400	4,500	1,600	1,200	54
21	1,600	280	37	<30	2,600	270	4,800	1,400	5,700	3,100	4,800	2,000	4,500	1,600	2,800	510	6,000	1,800	4,300	1,300	3,200	1,000	1,300	47
22	2,400	330	33	<30	2,300	360	4,700	1,800	6,500	3,300	4,200	1,800	4,600	1,700	2,300	560	6,000	1,800	4,500	1,400	3,900	980	2,700	110
23	1,800	370	230	<30	3,100	590	5,100	1,800	5,500	2,400	5,000	1,700	4,300	1,800	2,300	430	5,500	2,400	4,600	1,500	3,200	960	3,200	580
24	2,500	380	960	<30	3,700	570	5,900	2,200	4,900	2,400	5,200	1,800	4,300	1,700	2,900	460	6,200	2,100	3,700	1,300	3,200	800	3,500	450
25	3,700	660	1200	<30	3,600	580	6,900	2,800	3,800	2,000	5,200	1,900	4,200	1,600	2,900	530	5,500	2,400	3,900	1,300	3,600	690	3,400	490
26	3,500	920	1,300	<30	3,300	610	6,700	3,100	4,100	1,700	5,200	2,000	4,100	1,500	2,600	600	6,000	2,300	4,200	1,400	4,600	810	2,600	450
27	2,800	680	3,200	240	4,100	730	6,500	3,100	4,200	1,400	5,200	2,100	2,800	980	2,800	610	6,200	2,600	4,700	1,400	5,500	970	2,300	350
28	3,600	670	2,500	340	3,500	760	6,200	3,000	3,600	1,300	---	---	1,900	75	2,300	560	5,600	2,100	4,800	1,700	6,000	2,000	2,400	350
29	3,400	830	2,700	400			6,000	3,000	4,600	1,300	5,300	1,800	200	40	2,000	470	6,000	2,300	3,600	1,600	2,000	240	2,700	400
30	2,900	600	2,600	370			5,900	2,800	4,100	1,300	4,300	1,900	57	<30	2,500	470	5,800	3,100	4,800	1,300	1,200	91	2,100	390
31	3,000	590	3,000	510			5,500	2,800			4,800	2,100			2,800	570	5,500	2,800			2,300	84		
Mean	2,400	430	1,400	n.d.	2,300	410	4,700	1,800	5,300	2,500	5,200	2,100	4,400	n.d.	2,000	n.d.	5,700	2,000	4,800	1,900	4,200	1,300	2,400	320
Max	3,700	920	3,200	510	4,100	760	6,900	3,100	6,500	3,300	6,900	3,000	6,100	2,400	2,900	610	7,000	3,100	7,100	3,600	6,000	2,000	3,500	780
Min	840	110	33	<30	310	60	2,500	890	3,600	1,300	3,400	1,300	57	<30	45	<30	3,100	760	3,600	1,300	1,200	84	910	47

Table 18. Daily maximum and minimum chloride concentrations, Delaware River at Chester, Pennsylvania (station number 01477050), for report year ending November 30, 2006.

(Record furnished by Kimberly Clark Chester Operations)

[Concentrations in milligrams per liter; Max, maximum value; Min, minimum value]

DAY	DEC Max	DEC Min	JAN Max	JAN Min	FEB Max	FEB Min	MAR Max	MAR Min	APR Max	APR Min	MAY Max	MAY Min	JUNE Max	JUNE Min	JULY Max	JULY Min	AUG Max	AUG Min	SEPT Max	SEPT Min	OCT Max	OCT Min	NOV Max	NOV Min
1	31	27	46	38	28	28	53	46	54	44	46	33	36	28	27	18	28	22	64	61	28	28	31	31
2	31	31	36	36	28	28	53	53	54	46	39	39	36	36	33	22	28	22	64	36	28	28	31	31
3	31	27	36	28	28	28	43	37	61	54	46	33	44	28	33	22	28	22	44	36	36	28	31	25
4	31	21	54	28	28	22	54	54	61	53	46	33	36	32	33	33	36	36	44	36	36	28	31	25
5	31	31	36	36	28	28	53	53	61	53	46	33	36	28	33	33	36	36	36	28	36	28	31	25
6	31	31	36	28	28	28	53	53	54	53	33	33	36	28	33	33	36	36	36	28	36	28	31	25
7	31	31	36	31	28	28	53	53	68	61	44	33	36	28	33	33	36	36	36	28	39	33	31	31
8	31	31	36	36	28	28	53	50	61	53	40	33	36	28	33	33	36	36	36	28	39	33	31	31
9	31	31	36	36	28	28	53	53	61	53	39	33	28	28	28	28	36	28	38	34	39	39	36	31
10	31	31	36	28	28	28	57	46	61	53	39	33	28	28	33	33	36	28	44	36	39	33	33	33
11	36	36	36	28	28	21	61	53	63	53	39	33	28	28	33	22	28	28	36	28	33	33	33	33
12	36	31	36	28	28	20	53	50	53	53	33	33	28	28	28	22	28	28	36	36	53	38	33	33
13	31	27	36	28	37	28	54	44	53	53	33	33	28	28	28	22	36	36	36	36	33	33	33	30
14	36	36	36	28	37	28	54	44	53	53	36	33	36	28	33	27	54	44	36	36	33	33	42	30
15	36	31	36	36	43	37	54	44	53	53	46	46	28	28	33	27	54	54	36	28	33	33	36	31
16	64	49	36	28	43	37	54	44	54	54	53	46	36	28	33	20	54	54	36	20	33	33	36	31
17	36	36	36	28	57	43	54	54	53	53	46	33	28	28	33	20	54	54	36	28	39	33	36	31
18	54	44	36	28	65	50	54	44	61	53	39	33	36	28	33	20	54	54	36	28	39	33	36	31
19	54	54	28	22	43	43	44	36	53	53	39	33	28	26	28	20	54	54	36	28	39	33	36	31
20	54	54	36	28	43	43	44	44	69	53	39	33	28	28	28	20	64	54	36	28	33	33	31	31
21	54	54	28	20	57	46	44	44	61	53	46	33	28	28	28	22	64	54	36	28	33	33	36	36
22	54	54	28	28	53	46	44	44	61	53	39	33	28	28	36	22	64	54	40	28	37	31	71	63
23	54	54	28	28	53	46	44	44	61	53	39	33	36	28	28	28	54	44	36	28	37	31	31	31
24	54	54	28	20	53	46	54	36	61	53	36	33	39	33	28	28	64	64	36	28	33	33	31	31
25	54	54	28	20	53	53	54	44	53	53	39	36	39	28	36	26	108	74	36	28	33	33	31	31
26	54	54	28	20	53	46	54	22	53	46	39	33	50	39	36	28	120	85	28	28	25	25	31	31
27	54	44	28	20	53	46	54	44	53	53	39	33	39	33	33	28	120	85	28	28	31	31	31	31
28	54	54	28	22	53	53	44	44	46	39	39	33	39	33	33	28	120	64	28	28	31	31	37	31
29	44	54	28	22			64	54	46	39	39	39	39	33	33	28	114	64	28	28	31	31	36	31
30	44	54	28	28			54	44	46	33	39	39	21	20	33	28	114	74	28	28	31	28	31	31
31	44	54	28	28			54	54			36	28			28	23	74	54			31	31		
Mean	42	41	34	28	40	36	52	46	57	51	40	34	34	29	32	26	59	48	38	31	35	32	35	32
Max	64	54	54	38	65	53	64	54	69	61	53	46	50	39	36	33	120	85	64	61	53	39	71	63
Min	31	21	28	20	28	20	43	22	46	33	33	28	21	20	27	18	28	22	28	20	25	25	31	25

64

Table 19. Daily mean dissolved-oxygen concentration, Delaware River at Benjamin Franklin Bridge at Philadelphia, Pennsylvania (station number 01467200), April 1 to November 30, 2006.
(U.S. Geological Survey published record)

[Concentrations in milligrams per liter; Max, maximum value; Min, minimum value; ---, missing data]

DAY	APR	MAY	JUNE	JULY	AUG	SEPT	OCT	NOV
1	11.5	7.8	6.7	6.6	4.4	4.7	6.2	9.7
2	11.7	7.7	6.8	7.0	---	5.7	6.2	9.7
3	11.6	7.7	6.1	6.9	---	6.4	6.5	9.9
4	11.5	7.8	5.7	6.7	---	6.6	6.4	9.8
5	11.6	7.7	5.1	6.4	---	6.4	6.6	9.8
6	11.6	7.7	4.8	6.3	---	6.1	6.6	9.7
7	11.5	7.7	4.4	6.4	---	5.8	6.8	9.7
8	11.1	7.6	4.0	6.4	4.3	5.5	7.0	9.5
9	10.9	7.5	4.0	6.4	4.4	5.3	7.0	9.8
10	10.6	7.1	4.3	6.4	4.4	5.2	6.8	9.7
11	10.2	6.7	4.8	6.3	4.3	5.2	6.6	8.8
12	9.6	---	4.9	6.1	4.3	5.1	6.3	8.5
13	9.1	---	4.9	6.0	4.3	5.0	6.6	8.4
14	8.9	---	4.9	6.0	4.3	4.9	6.8	8.5
15	8.6	---	5.0	6.1	4.5	4.8	6.8	8.7
16	8.5	6.2	5.1	5.9	4.4	5.1	6.8	8.6
17	8.5	6.4	5.3	5.7	4.5	5.6	6.7	8.4
18	8.4	6.5	5.6	5.5	4.4	6.2	6.5	8.8
19	8.3	6.5	5.9	5.4	4.4	6.7	6.6	8.6
20	8.3	6.8	5.9	5.5	4.5	6.8	6.6	8.7
21	8.5	7.1	5.8	5.3	4.5	7.0	6.9	9.1
22	8.5	7.4	5.6	5.2	4.6	6.9	7.4	9.6
23	8.1	7.4	5.4	5.1	4.5	6.8	7.6	9.9
24	7.8	7.3	5.1	4.7	4.5	6.7	8.0	10.2
25	7.4	7.4	5.0	4.6	4.3	6.4	8.2	10.6
26	6.9	7.1	4.7	4.8	4.2	6.2	8.3	10.6
27	7.0	7.0	4.6	4.8	4.2	6.1	8.5	10.6
28	7.3	7.3	5.3	4.8	4.3	6.0	8.5	10.6
29	7.5	7.2	5.8	4.6	3.9	6.1	9.5	10.6
30	7.7	7.2	6.3	4.5	3.7	6.2	9.8	10.6
31		6.8		4.4	3.9		9.6	
Mean	9.3	7.2	5.3	5.7	4.3	5.9	7.2	9.5
Max	11.7	7.8	6.8	7.0	4.6	7.0	9.8	10.6
Min	6.9	6.2	4.0	4.4	3.7	4.7	6.2	8.4

Table 20. Daily mean dissolved-oxygen concentration, Delaware River at Chester, Pennsylvania (station number 01477050), April 1 to November 30, 2006. (U.S. Geological Survey published record)

[Concentrations in milligrams per liter; Max, maximum value; Min, minimum value; ---, missing data]

DAY	APR	MAY	JUNE	JULY	AUG	SEPT	OCT	NOV
1	9.9	6.9	6.5	7.1	5.0	5.6	6.4	9.7
2	9.7	6.9	6.4	7.1	4.8	6.7	6.4	9.8
3	9.4	7.0	6.0	7.0	4.6	6.0	6.2	10.0
4	9.4	7.0	5.6	6.8	4.6	5.7	6.0	10.1
5	9.5	7.0	5.5	6.6	4.6	5.7	6.1	10.1
6	9.5	7.1	5.5	6.6	4.8	5.7	6.4	10.1
7	9.3	7.2	5.4	6.4	5.0	5.5	---	---
8	---	7.3	5.2	6.1	5.0	5.2	---	---
9	---	7.6	4.9	5.9	5.0	5.2	---	---
10	---	7.4	4.8	5.9	5.2	5.2	---	9.5
11	9.0	7.4	5.1	5.7	5.4	5.5	---	9.4
12	8.8	7.5	5.2	5.5	5.4	5.8	6.9	9.5
13	8.7	7.1	5.1	5.4	5.3	5.8	7.0	9.6
14	8.4	6.9	4.9	5.2	5.5	5.8	7.1	9.3
15	8.0	7.0	4.7	5.1	5.7	5.7	7.3	8.8
16	7.9	6.5	4.7	4.8	5.6	5.4	7.3	8.8
17	7.7	6.3	4.7	4.8	5.5	5.4	7.5	9.0
18	7.6	6.1	4.8	4.7	5.1	5.4	7.5	9.2
19	7.5	5.8	4.9	4.7	5.0	5.4	7.0	9.2
20	7.4	6.0	5.1	4.8	5.2	5.5	---	9.6
21	7.5	6.2	5.0	4.7	5.3	5.8	---	10.0
22	8.0	6.5	4.9	4.8	5.3	5.8	---	10.0
23	7.9	6.6	4.8	4.8	5.2	6.0	---	10.4
24	7.3	6.6	4.8	4.6	5.2	6.0	9.0	10.6
25	6.9	6.5	4.6	4.7	5.2	6.2	8.8	10.8
26	6.9	6.3	4.8	4.6	5.4	6.3	8.8	10.9
27	6.8	6.1	5.3	4.7	5.6	6.3	8.4	11.2
28	6.7	6.0	5.6	4.8	5.5	6.3	8.8	11.2
29	6.6	6.1	6.3	4.9	5.0	6.5	9.6	11.2
30	6.7	6.1	7.0	4.9	4.8	6.5	9.8	11.2
31		6.3		4.9	4.8		9.7	
Mean	8.1	6.7	5.3	5.4	5.1	5.8	7.6	10.0
Max	9.9	7.6	7.0	7.1	5.7	6.7	9.8	11.2
Min	6.6	5.8	4.6	4.6	4.6	5.2	6.0	8.8

Appendix A

Rainfall Event Based
Temporary Spill Reduction Program
for
Pepacton Reservoir
February 8, 2006

On April 21, 2004, the Parties to the 1954 U.S. Supreme Court Decree (Decree Parties) approved an interim program for managing releases from the New York City Delaware Basin reservoirs. That interim program was embodied in Delaware River Basin Commission (DRBC) Resolution No. 2004-3 Docket No. D-77-20 (Revision 7). In approving that resolution, the Decree Parties committed to continuing discussions to develop and implement by May 31, 2007 a long-term flexible program to manage releases from the City Delaware Basin reservoirs to better address fisheries in the tailwaters below those reservoirs; the Decree Parties agreed that implementation of such a program required consideration of other related issues.

The Decree Parties agree that reduction of Pepacton Reservoir spill during flood events is a related issue that should be considered in the development of the long-term flexible program. The Decree Parties also agree that reduction of Pepacton Reservoir spill should not be delayed until final approval of a long-term flexible program occurs, and hereby agree to implement a temporary spill reduction program for the period ending March 31, 2006.

During active hydrologic conditions that result in full or nearly full storage in Pepacton Reservoir and overall in the New York City (NYC) Delaware Basin Reservoirs, the temporary spill reduction program described below will be implemented to reduce the volume of water spilled from Pepacton Reservoir. The program will attempt to manage a storage void to completely capture runoff produced by a one inch rainfall event, based on the National Weather Service's Upper Delaware Basin Water Supply Guidance for the reservoir's watershed (see sample guidance statement at 7., below), through supplemental releases above normal conservation rates from the East Delaware Release Chamber. The void shall be maintained during the period ending March 31, 2006. This temporary program is not part of any regular release program and does not establish a precedent for any future releases or actions.

Although the total volume of water spilled from Pepacton Reservoir may be reduced by this temporary program, it is unlikely that peak flows downstream will be significantly reduced. Pepacton Reservoir provides substantial attenuation of peak flows downstream even when the reservoir is spilling. The reservoir was not designed as a flood control reservoir and does not contain release works capable of releasing water at rates necessary for effective flood management operation; consequently, the Decree Parties continue to strongly urge communities downstream of the reservoir to take all necessary and prudent actions to improve flood preparedness and increase awareness of flood potential.

Temporary Pepacton Reservoir Spill Reduction Program:

1. Upon approval of this agreement by the Decree Parties, the City of New York will implement a temporary program to achieve limited reduction of Pepacton Reservoir storage through supplemental releases from the East Delaware Release Chamber.

2. For the period ending March 31, 2006, whenever the void in Pepacton Reservoir is less than the expected runoff volume that would result from a one inch rainfall event as predicted by the National Weather Service's Upper Delaware Basin Water Supply Guidance, supplemental releases will be made as necessary to maintain to the extent practicable, a void sufficient to completely capture the runoff volume forecasted for a one inch rainfall event.

3. The recommended rate of the supplemental release shall be established daily by NYC in consultation with the Delaware River Master. Releases above the normal conservation rate will be accounted for as

special releases and be considered neither River Master directed releases nor conservation releases in accordance with DRBC Docket D-77-20 (Revision 7).

4. The River Master will manage the recommended supplemental releases in such a manner as to conserve the waters of the Delaware Basin in accordance with the following guidance:

    i. The flood stage for the East Branch Delaware River at Fishs Eddy is 13 feet. Accordingly, supplemental releases will not be made when the river stage for the East Branch Delaware River at Fishs Eddy is above 11 feet, or is forecasted to be above 11 feet within 48 hours of a planned supplemental release from Pepacton Reservoir. This guidance may be modified at any time if additional information demonstrates that a lower cautionary stage should be used to limit the supplemental releases.

    ii. Supplemental releases may be suspended if ice conditions threaten flood prone areas of the East Branch Delaware River below Pepacton Reservoir.

    iii. Supplemental releases will be designed so that the combined discharge from the East Delaware Release Chamber and the Downsville Dam spillway does not exceed 2,000 cubic feet per second (cfs). All supplemental releases will be discontinued when the spillway discharge exceeds 2,000 cfs.

5. This temporary program will be run concurrently with the existing snowpack-based spill reduction program. Voids maintained under the two programs shall not be additive.

6. If releases are made pursuant to this program and Pepacton Reservoir fails to reach 99% storage prior to the start of drawdown, the difference between the actual reservoir storage at the start of drawdown and the full capacity of the reservoir will be deducted from NYC's authorized Delaware Basin diversion for the upcoming hydrological year (i.e., year beginning June 1, 2006).

7. Example of National Weather Service Product:

    http ://www.srh.noaa.gov/productview.php?pil=FFHPA2

    UPPER DELAWARE BASIN WATER SUPPLY GUIDANCE

    APPROXIMATE RUNOFF (IN MILLIONS OF GALLONS) PRODUCED FROM EACH OF THE FOLLOWING 6-HOUR RAINFALL AMOUNTS (IN INCHES):

: :IDENT	0.1	0.5	**RAINFALL** **1.0**	2.0	3.0	5.0	**LOCATION**
======	=====	=====	=====	=====	=====	=====	===============
CANN6DEL	470/	2398/	4833/	10303/	16190/	27962	:CANNONSVILLE
DWNN6DEL	422/	2237/	4590/	9857/	15318/	26238	: PEPACTON
NVRN6NVR	28/	311/	666/	1494/	2459/	4403	:NEVERSINK
.END							
$$							

8. This agreement will expire on May 31, 2007 and may be terminated at any time at the request of any Decree Party or may be modified with the unanimous consent of the Decree Parties.

Consent to Action by The City of New York

Consent of the Parties to the U.S. Supreme Court Decree in <u>New Jersey v. New York</u>, 347 U.S. 995 (1954), approving the Pepacton Reservoir Temporary Spill Reduction Program, February 8, 2006 through May 31, 2007, implemented by the City of New York.

State of New Jersey	Date		State of New York	Date

State of Delaware	Date		Commonwealth of Pennsylvania	Date

State of Delaware	Date		City of New York	Date

Appendix B

Rainfall Event Based
Temporary Spill Reduction Program
for
Neversink Reservoir
February 8, 2006

On April 21, 2004, the Parties to the 1954 U.S. Supreme Court Decree (Decree Parties) approved an interim program for managing releases from the New York City Delaware Basin reservoirs. That interim program was embodied in Delaware River Basin Commission (DRBC) Resolution No. 2004-3 Docket No. D-77-20 (Revision 7). In approving that resolution, the Decree Parties committed to continuing discussions to develop and implement by May 31, 2007 a long-term flexible program to manage releases from the City Delaware Basin reservoirs to better address fisheries in the tailwaters below those reservoirs; the Decree Parties agreed that implementation of such a program required consideration of other related issues.

The Decree Parties agree that reduction of Neversink Reservoir spill during flood events is a related issue that should be considered in the development of the long-term flexible program. The Decree Parties also agree that reduction of Neversink Reservoir spill should not be delayed until final approval of a long-term flexible program occurs, and hereby agree to implement a temporary spill reduction program for the period ending March 31, 2006.

During active hydrologic conditions that result in full or nearly full storage in Neversink Reservoir and overall in the New York City (NYC) Delaware Basin Reservoirs, the temporary spill reduction program described below will be implemented to reduce the volume of water spilled from Neversink Reservoir. The program will attempt to manage a storage void to completely capture runoff produced by a one inch rainfall event, based on the National Weather Service's Upper Delaware Basin Water Supply Guidance for the reservoir's watershed (see sample guidance statement at 7., below), through supplemental releases above normal conservation rates from the Neversink Release Chamber. The void shall be maintained during the period ending March 31, 2006. This temporary program is not part of any regular release program and does not establish a precedent for any future releases or actions.

Although the total volume of water spilled from Neversink Reservoir may be reduced by this temporary program, it is unlikely that peak flows downstream will be significantly reduced. Neversink Reservoir provides substantial attenuation of peak flows downstream even when the reservoir is spilling. The reservoir was not designed as a flood control reservoir and does not contain release works capable of releasing water at rates necessary for effective flood management operation; consequently, the Decree Parties continue to strongly urge communities downstream of the reservoir to take all necessary and prudent actions to improve flood preparedness and increase awareness of flood potential.

Temporary Neversink Reservoir Spill Reduction Program:

1. Upon approval of this agreement by the Decree Parties, the City of New York will implement a temporary program to achieve limited reduction of Neversink Reservoir storage through supplemental releases from the Neversink Release Chamber.

2. For the period ending March 31, 2006, whenever the void in Neversink Reservoir is less than the expected runoff volume that would result from a one inch rainfall event as predicted by the National Weather Service's Upper Delaware Basin Water Supply Guidance, supplemental releases will be made as necessary to maintain to the extent practicable, a void sufficient to completely capture the runoff volume forecasted for a one inch rainfall event.

3. The recommended rate of the supplemental release shall be established daily by NYC in consultation with the Delaware River Master. Releases above the normal conservation rate will be accounted for as special releases and be considered neither River Master directed releases nor conservation releases in accordance with DRBC Docket D-77-20 (Revision 7).

4. The River Master will manage the recommended supplemental releases in such a manner as to conserve the waters of the Delaware Basin in accordance with the following guidance:

   i. The flood stage for the Neversink River at Bridgeville is 8 feet. Accordingly, supplemental releases will not be made when the river stage for the Neversink River at Bridgeville is above 6 feet, or is forecasted to be above 6 feet within 48 hours of a planned supplemental release from Neversink Reservoir. This guidance may be modified at any time if additional information demonstrates that a lower cautionary stage should be used to limit the supplemental releases.

   ii. Supplemental releases may be suspended if ice conditions threaten flood prone areas of the Neversink River below Neversink Reservoir.

   iii. Supplemental releases will be designed so that the combined discharge from the Neversink Release Chamber and the Neversink Dam spillway does not exceed 750 cubic feet per second (cfs). All supplemental releases will be discontinued when the spillway discharge exceeds 750 cfs.

5. This temporary program will be run concurrently with the existing snowpack-based spill reduction program. Voids maintained under the two programs shall not be additive.

6. If releases are made pursuant to this program and Neversink Reservoir fails to reach 99% storage prior to the start of drawdown, the difference between the actual reservoir storage at the start of drawdown and the full capacity of the reservoir will be deducted from NYC's authorized Delaware Basin diversion for the upcoming hydrological year (i.e., year beginning June 1, 2006).

7. Example of National Weather Service Product:

   http ://www.srh.noaa.gov/productview.php?pil=FFHPA2

   UPPER DELAWARE BASIN WATER SUPPLY GUIDANCE

   APPROXIMATE RUNOFF (IN MILLIONS OF GALLONS) PRODUCED FROM EACH OF THE FOLLOWING 6-HOUR RAINFALL AMOUNTS (IN INCHES):

:			**RAINFALL**				
:IDENT	0.1	0.5	**1.0**	2.0	3.0	5.0	**LOCATION**
======	=====	=====	=====	=====	=====	=====	===============
CANN6DEL	470/	2398/	4833/	10303/	16190/	27962	:CANNONSVILLE
DWNN6DEL	422/	2237/	4590/	9857/	15318/	26238	: PEPACTON
NVRN6NVR	28/	311/	666/	1494/	2459/	4403	:NEVERSINK
.END							
$$							

8. This agreement will expire on May 31, 2007 and may be terminated at any time at the request of any Decree Party or may be modified with the unanimous consent of the Decree Parties.

Consent to Action by The City of New York

Consent of the Parties to the U.S. Supreme Court Decree in <u>New Jersey v. New York</u>, 347 U.S. 995 (1954), approving the Neversink Reservoir Temporary Spill Reduction Program, February 8, 2006 through May 31, 2007, implemented by the City of New York.

State of New Jersey	Date	State of New York	Date
State of Delaware	Date	Commonwealth of Pennsylvania	Date
State of Delaware	Date	City of New York	Date

Appendix C

NO. 2006-18
DOCKET NO. D-77-20 CP (Revision 9)

A RESOLUTION supplementing and amending Docket No. D-77-20 CP (Revisions 7 and 8) to establish a temporary spill mitigation program for Neversink, Pepacton and Cannonsville Reservoirs.

WHEREAS, on April 21, 2004, the Delaware River Basin Commission (DRBC) with the unanimous consent of the Parties to the 1954 Supreme Court Decree (Decree Parties) adopted Resolution No. 2004-3, Docket No. D-77-20 CP (Revision 7), establishing an interim program for managing releases from the New York City Neversink, Pepacton and Cannonsville Reservoirs (NYC Delaware Basin Reservoirs);

WHEREAS, on July 13, 2004, the DRBC adopted Resolution No. 2004-9, Docket No. D-77-20 CP (Revision 8), amending Docket No. D-77-20 CP (Revision 7) to allow a portion of the Excess Release Quantity established by the 1954 Supreme Court Decree to be used for purposes of aquatic resource research related to fisheries enhancement, including dwarf wedgemussel studies;

WHEREAS, through Resolution No. 2004-3 the Decree Parties committed to continuing discussions to develop and implement by May 31, 2007 a long-term flexible program to manage releases from the NYC Delaware Basin Reservoirs to better address fisheries and other needs in the tailwaters below these reservoirs;

WHEREAS, in Resolution No. 2004-3 the Decree Parties agreed that the long-term program must take into account related issues including but not limited to those issues specified in this Resolution;

WHEREAS, reduction of spill volumes from the NYC Delaware Basin Reservoirs during flood events is a related issue under consideration in the development of the long-term flexible program;

WHEREAS, the Commission and Decree Parties believe that implementation of a temporary spill mitigation program through May 31, 2007 may reduce excess spillage through supplemental releases from the NYC Delaware Basin Reservoirs and should not be delayed until final approval of a long-term flexible program occurs;

WHEREAS, the NYC Delaware Basin Reservoirs already provide substantial attenuation of peak flows downstream even when one or more of the reservoirs is spilling; and

WHEREAS, an interim spill mitigation program has the potential to reduce spill rates and offer a small measure of peak flow reduction during a flood event, although any such reduction will diminish with increasing distance downstream of the Cannonsville, Pepacton, and Neversink dams;

WHEREAS, the NYC Delaware Basin Reservoirs were not designed as flood control reservoirs and do not contain release works capable of releasing water at rates necessary for effective flood management operation;

WHEREAS, notwithstanding this temporary spill mitigation program the DRBC and the Decree Parties strongly encourage communities and individuals downstream of the NYC Delaware Basin Reservoirs to take all necessary and prudent actions to improve flood preparedness and increase awareness of flood potential;

WHEREAS, in light of the only limited flood mitigation benefits achievable through this spill mitigation program and the benefits to the Basin community from better flood management information and flood control, through a concurrent resolution Pennsylvania, New Jersey, New York and Delaware have agreed to share the cost of developing a model to study more broadly and thoroughly the potential effects of managing reservoirs throughout the Basin to reduce flooding in the Delaware River and its tributaries;

WHEREAS, the Commission intends to form a task force to examine stormwater management, land-use patterns, open space and farmland preservation, floodplain regulations and other potential non-structural flood mitigation measures in the Basin; and

WHEREAS, New York City with the consent of the other Decree Parties commenced implementation of a temporary spill mitigation program on September 22, 2006, subject to further action by the DRBC; now therefore

BE IT RESOLVED by the undersigned Commissioners and Decree Parties:

1. For the period ending May 31, 2007, whenever the usable storage in the NYC Delaware Basin Reservoirs is above the 80% rule curve as shown in Figure 1, in lieu of the releases otherwise required under Docket D-77-20 (Revision 7), supplemental releases from the NYC Delaware Basin Reservoirs will be made in accordance with the individual rule curves shown on Figure 2 and at rates as shown in Table 1. In order to provide for such releases, it is agreed that the operational assumptions used for modeling analyses and stipulated in paragraph 2 will apply throughout the period this program remains in effect.

2. The releases under this program have been modeled using the OASIS model and are based upon an operational assumption of a running daily average diversion by the City of not more than 610 mgd, combined, from the NYC Delaware Basin Reservoirs. The habitat flow targets, in accordance with Revision 7, continue to apply when storage is above the 80% rule curve.

Figure 1

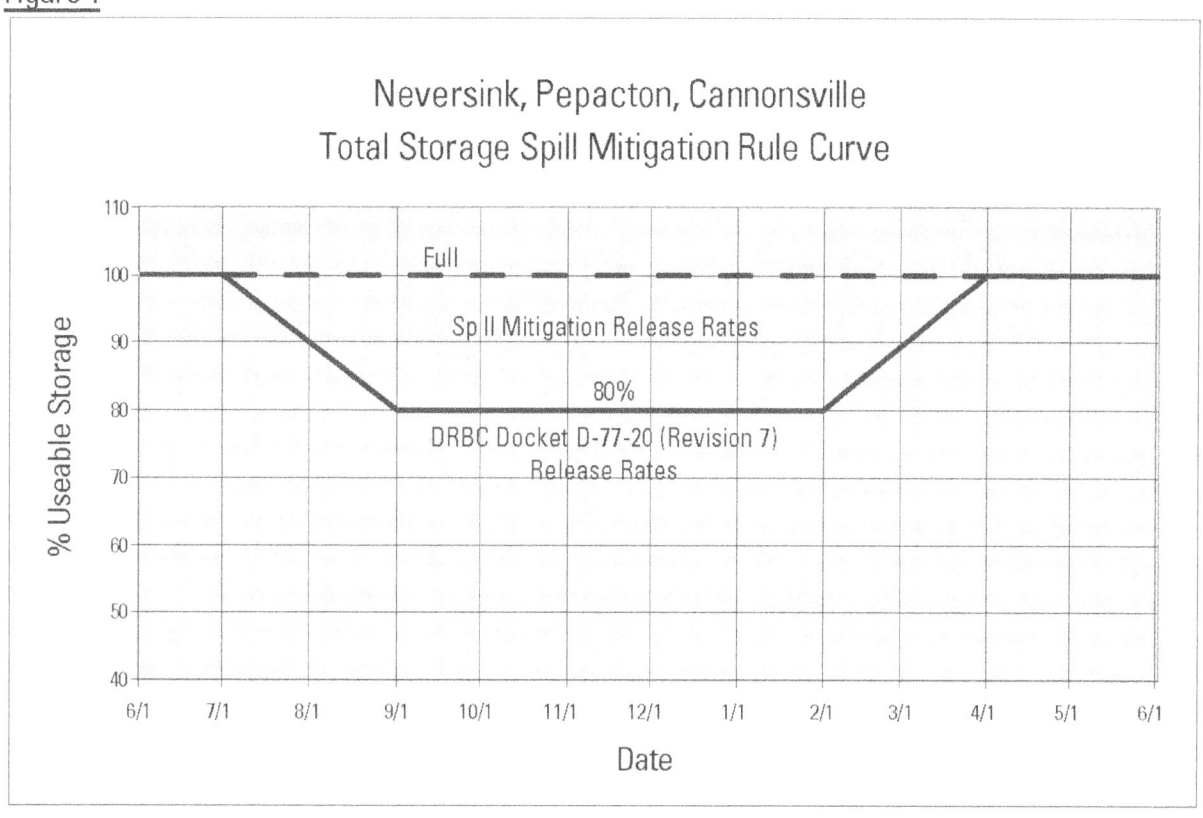

Neversink, Pepacton, Cannonsville
Total Storage Spill Mitigation Rule Curve

Figure 2

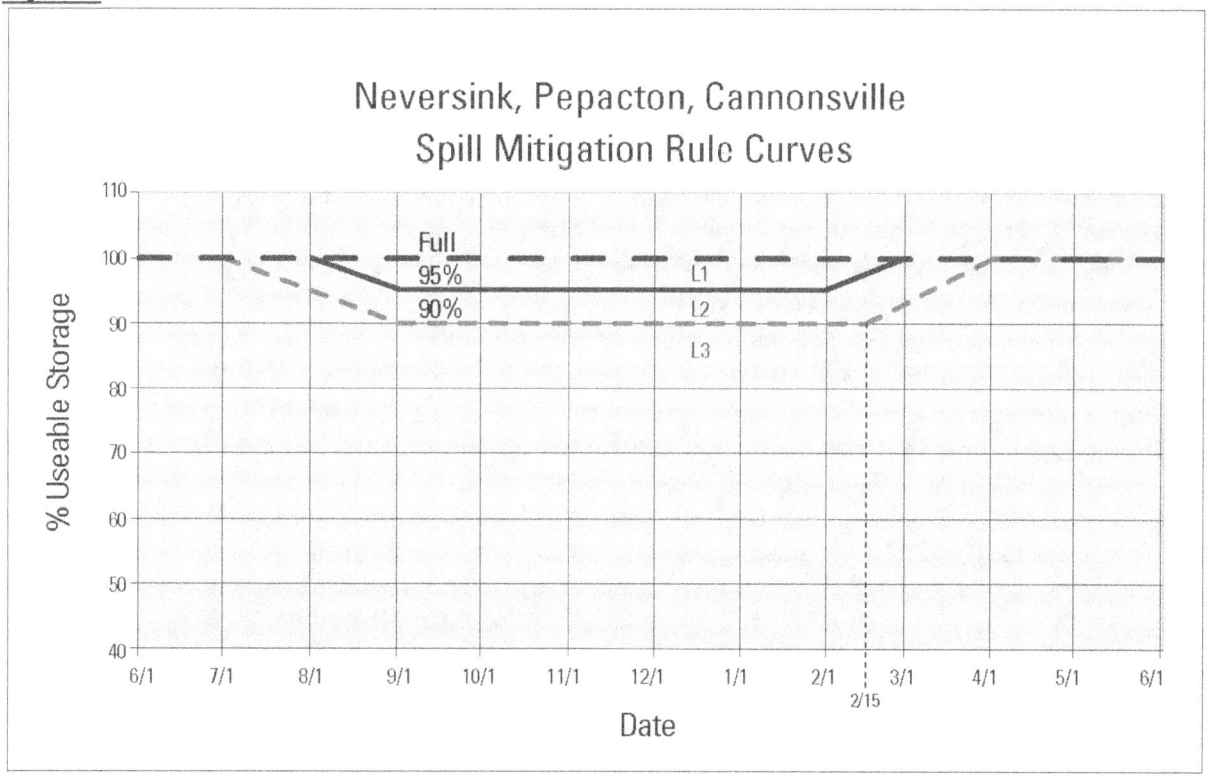

Neversink, Pepacton, Cannonsville
Spill Mitigation Rule Curves

Table 1

Release Level	Release Rates (cfs)					
	Spring/Fall			Winter		
	Cannonsville	Pepacton	Neversink	Cannonsville	Pepacton	Neversink
L1	1000	700	190	1000	700	190
L2	275	200	85	250	185	85
L3	140	100	75	110	85	65

Spring/Fall:	May 1 - May 31 and Sept 15 - Sept 30
Winter:	October 1 - April 30

3. Controlled reservoir releases will be made in accordance with the following:

   i. The flood stage for the West Branch Delaware River at Hale Eddy is 11 feet. Accordingly, supplemental releases from Cannonsville Reservoir will not be made when the river stage for the West Branch Delaware River at Hale Eddy is above 9 feet, or is forecasted to be above 9 feet within 48 hours of a planned supplemental release from Cannonsville Reservoir. This guidance may be modified at any time if additional information demonstrates that a lower cautionary stage should be used to limit the supplemental releases.

   ii. The flood stage for the East Branch Delaware River at Fishs Eddy is 15.0 ft. Accordingly, supplemental releases will not be made when the river stage for the East Branch Delaware River at Fishs Eddy is above 13.0 ft. or is forecast to be above 13.0 ft. within 48 hours of a planned supplemental release from Pepacton Reservoir. This guidance may be modified at any time if additional information demonstrates that a lower cautionary stage should be used to limit the supplemental releases.

   iii. The flood stage for the Neversink River at Bridgeville is 8 feet. Accordingly, supplemental releases will not be made when the river stage for the Neversink River at Bridgeville is above 6 feet, or is forecast to be above 6 feet within 48 hours of a planned supplemental release from Neversink Reservoir. This guidance may be modified at any time if additional information demonstrates that a lower cautionary stage should be used to limit the supplemental releases.

   iv. Supplemental releases may be suspended from the respective reservoir if ice conditions threaten flood prone areas of the Neversink River below Neversink Reservoir, East Branch Delaware River below Pepacton Reservoir, or West Branch Delaware River below Cannonsville Reservoir.

   v. Supplemental releases will be designed so that the combined discharge from the reservoirs and their respective spillways do not exceed flow rates as detailed in Table 2 below. All controlled releases will be reduced to the conservation releases in Table 3 when the spillway discharge exceeds these flow rates.

   vi. To more naturally effect downward transitions between release levels identified in Figures 1 and 2 and Table 1, supplemental release rates shall be ramped generally over a three-day period at Cannonsville and Pepacton Reservoirs and a two-day period at Neversink Reservoir, but in increments no less than 10 cfs at any reservoir.

Table 2

Reservoir	Maximum Combined Spill/Release Flow Rate
Neversink	1800 cfs
Pepacton	2400 cfs
Cannonsville	2200 cfs

Table 3

Conservation Releases

Reservoir	Conservation Release (cfs)			
	Drought Normal	Drought Watch	Warning	Drought
Cannonsville (9/1 - 5/31)	45	38	32	23
Cannonsville (6/1 - 8/31)	60	51	43	23
Pepacton	35	30	25	19
Neversink	25	21	18	15

4. For the period ending May 31, 2007, whenever the total storage in the NYC Delaware Basin Reservoirs is below the applicable point on the 80% rule curve as shown in Figure 1, releases from the NYC Delaware Basin Reservoirs will be made and accounted for in accordance with DRBC Docket D-77-20 (Revision 7).

5. For the period ending May 31, 2007, whenever the total storage in the NYC Delaware Basin Reservoirs is above the applicable point on the 80% rule curve as shown in Figure 1 and supplemental releases are made in accordance with this spill mitigation program, to the extent necessary, habitat releases may be made to meet the habitat flow targets in accordance with DRBC Docket D-77-20 (Revision 7). There shall be no credits or debits to the 'Habitat Protection Bank' as established in Revision 7 including without limitation to the Excess Release Quantity Bank portion of the Habitat Protection Bank provided from the Excess Release Quantity.

6. The "Rainfall Event Based Temporary Spill Reduction Program for Pepacton Reservoir" effective February 8, 2006 and "Rainfall Event Based Temporary Spill Reduction Program for Neversink Reservoir" effective February 8, 2006 are hereby suspended for the effective period of this agreement.

7. The "Interim Program for Neversink Reservoir Spill Reduction" effective November 1, 2005 and the "Interim Program for Pepacton Reservoir Spill Reduction" effective November 1, 2005 are hereby suspended for the effective period of this agreement.

8. A quantity of water no greater than 50% of the water equivalent of snow pack storage in the watershed above each reservoir will be included in the storage calculation to determine the reservoir release levels in Figure 2 and Table 1.

9. The actions of New York City commencing implementation of the spill mitigation program with the agreement of the other Decree Parties are ratified and approved.

10. The program established by this Resolution will expire on May 31, 2007 and may be terminated at any time by the Commission or at the request of any Decree Party or may be modified by the Commission with the unanimous consent of the Decree Parties.

/s/ Gwen E. Baker
Lt. Col. Gwen E Baker, Chair *pro tem*

/s/ Pamela M. Bush
Pamela M. Bush, Esq., Commission Secretary

ADOPTED: September 27, 2006

Consent to Action by the Decree Parties

Consent of the Parties to the U.S. Supreme Court Decree in <u>New Jersey v. New York</u>, 347 U.S. 995 (1954), approving the Temporary Spill Mitigation Program for Neversink, Pepacton and Cannonsville Reservoirs, September 27, 2006 through May 31, 2007, implemented by the City of New York.

/s/ Samuel A. Wolfe 9/27/06		/s/ Fred Nuffer 9/27/06
State of New Jersey Date		State of New York Date

/s/ Samuel A. Wolfe   9/27/06
State of New Jersey   Date

/s/ Fred Nuffer   9/27/06
State of New York   Date

/s/ John H. Talley   9/27/06
State of Delaware   Date

/s/ Cathy Curran Myers   9/27/06
Commonwealth of Pennsylvania   Date

/s/ Harry W. Otto   9/27/06
State of Delaware   Date

/s/ Michael A. Principe   9/27/06
City of New York   Date

≋USGS

Krejmas, Bruce E., Paulachok, Gary N., and Blanchard, Stephen F.—**Report of the River Master of the Delaware River**—Open-File Report 2011–1177